W9-CLC-947

Awakening the Academy

Awakening the Academy

A Time for New Leadership

Wellford W. Wilms
University of California, Los Angeles

Deone M. Zell
California State University, Northridge

ANKER PUBLISHING COMPANY, INC.
Bolton, Massachusetts

Awakening the Academy
A Time for New Leadership

ISBN 1-882982-48-7

Composition by Vicki Czech
Cover design by Vicki Czech

Anker Publishing Company, Inc.
176 Ballville Road
P.O. Box 249
Bolton, MA 01740-0249   USA

www.ankerpub.com

To Ben

Table of Contents

About the Authors

Wellford W. Wilms is a professor in UCLA's Graduate School of Education and Information Studies where he is faculty director of its Educational Leadership Program. He has served as chair of the faculty and assistant dean for student affairs. He also holds an appointment in UCLA's School of Public Policy and Social Research.

For over a decade, Wilms has conducted action research to understand organizations' adaptive strategies and provided them with feedback to help them to manage in changing environments. Results of a five-year study of private sector organizations were published in 1996 in the book *Restoring Prosperity: How Manager and Workers are Forging a New Culture of Cooperation* by Times Books, Random House.

More recently, Wilms has extended his interests to the public sector—the Los Angeles Police Department (LAPD), public schools and teacher unions, and higher education. He is currently writing a book on change in the LAPD. His research is supported by the National Institute of Justice, the Alfred P. Sloan Foundation, the John and Dora Haynes Foundation, and the Pew Charitable Trusts.

Wilms serves on a number of editorial boards and as an advisor to the Social Sciences Research Council, UCLA's Human Resources Round Table, United Teachers Los Angeles Helen Bernstein Professional Development Center, and the Center for Research and Innovation in Society. He also serves as a mediator for the Los Angeles City Attorney's Dispute Resolution Program.

Deone M. Zell is an assistant professor, Department of Management, California State University, Northridge, where she teaches courses in management, organizational theory and change. For the last decade, she has been using qualitative research methods to study how organizations adapt to changing environments. She conducted a multiyear, in-depth investigation of organizational change at Hewlett-Packard, the results of which were published by Cornell University Press in 1997 in a book titled *Changing by Design: Organizational Innovation at Hewlett-Packard*.

More recently, Zell has conducted research in the areas of knowledge management, complexity theory, organizational adaptation, and the diffusion of innovations. Results of her research have been published in the *Sloan Management Review*, *Organizational Dynamics*, and the *Journal of Management Inquiry*. Currently she is working on several research projects including a study of strategic planning and management in large private and public sector organizations, the diffusion of a teaching innovation throughout a large public school district, and the nature of strategic change in professional organizations such as consulting firms, hospitals, and universities.

Preface

When we began writing this book in 2000, we had become keenly aware of the difficulty facing colleges and universities as they try to adjust to a changing environment. Our study of the University of California, Los Angeles (UCLA), on which this book is based, gave ample testimony about how a large research university responds to external demands while safeguarding the very qualities that make a university such a special place. Members of our research team, and our benefactors at the Alfred P. Sloan Foundation, were surprised and heartened by the finding that when life or death decisions had to be made, the faculty and administration acted wisely and in concert with one another.

But does it take a crisis to change? We think not. As this book shows, when the faculty becomes seriously engaged in identifying problems and searching for solutions, things change. But engaging the faculty in planning for the university's welfare is another matter. So much of what passes for strategic planning falls on deaf ears when it reaches the faculty, the result of a number of factors that we take up in this book. Engaging the faculty will require nothing less than rethinking established governance arrangements that have successfully insulated the faculty from feeling pressures for change. While insulating the faculty may have been well intentioned and rational in a static environment, it has serious drawbacks today. Beset by competing demands and scarce resources, universities and colleges have to make hard choices. But if these decisions are to be good ones and if they are to be durable, faculties must be engaged in their making.

Organization of this Book

We have organized the book to lead the reader from the topsy-turvy environment of higher education described in Chapter One into a detailed examination of UCLA through the lenses of its own administrative apparatus in Chapter Two. Next, in Chapters Three, Four, and Five we put the microscope on three significant academic units to show how they respond. We spent the better part of four years with our research team digging into these units using an unusually wide array of research tools ranging from interviews and observations to social network and process mapping, time budgets, and financial analyses. We triangulated this massive body of data to ensure that reported findings from one data source were not contradicted by another. Along the way we subjected the findings to scrutiny by faculty leaders and administrators to verify their accuracy. Chapter Six draws these findings into a set of conclusions to help academic leaders think differently about their institutions.

We have avoided offering simplified prescriptions about what administrators or faculty leaders should or must do. Instead we hope to persuade readers on the basis of our evidence that change without crisis is possible. In the course of this study we have become convinced that colleges and universities can actually learn from their environment and make strategic adaptations, despite the heavy armor developed over centuries designed to produce just the opposite.

The book concludes with a number of specific recommendations about steps that can be taken to make the process of change less of a knee-jerk reaction to a seamless and continuous process of adaptation and improvement. Among them is the recommendation that feedback from students, alumni, and other influential actors be channeled back into the university's core processes—teaching, research, and public service—to help guide the process of improvement and cultural change. This observation is based on the knowledge that cultural change is the product of creative adaptation to external reality. Our research on industrial change revealed how successful companies and unions altered their core processes in the expectation that productive cultures would follow. Our hope is to provoke new ideas among academic leaders about creative ways to enlist their faculties in the processes of change at this critical time in the history of higher education.

Acknowledgements

We wish to acknowledge a number of individuals whose contributions made this book possible. First, our UCLA research partners C. Kumar Patel, former vice chancellor of research and professor of physics, and Uday S. Karmarkar, Times Mirror, professor in the Anderson School. Thanks also to Gayle Byock, assistant vice chancellor, UCLA, for her support and good humor. We are grateful for the hard work of members of the research team—Cheryl Teruya, Karen McClafferty, Suzanne Stauffer, MaryBeth Walpole, Nabil Abu-Ghazaleh, Mark Wittenberg, Don Chisholm, and Tuyen Hoang—who spent long hours gathering and analyzing data. Thanks also to Claudia Lopez, administrative assistant in UCLA's Educational Leadership Program for logistical help. We also appreciate the support of the deans and chairs and faculty members of the academic units under study, who reviewed our work as it progressed and provided valuable commentary on earlier drafts.

For the transformation of the study into a book manuscript, we wish to acknowledge the contributions of Elsa Dixler, Director of Publications, the Social Science Research Council; Patricia Gumport, Professor of Education, Stanford University; John Hawkins, former Dean of International Studies and Mike Rose, Professor of Education at UCLA. We wish to acknowledge the roles of UCLA professors of higher education, Helen Astin and Alexander Astin for a stimulating and long-standing conversation about the nature of change in higher education.

We also wish to thank the Alfred P. Sloan Foundation for its generous support, and to acknowledge the leadership of program director Jesse Ausubel, who foresaw the significance of the changes taking place in higher education. Finally, thanks to our editors, Tara Freeman, editorial assistant, and Susan Anker, vice president of Anker Publishing Company.

Wellford W. Wilms
Deone M. Zell

September 2001

Navigating in Uncertainty

Changes that have transformed the global economy are now sweeping through higher education. Rising costs, uncertain revenues, exponential growth in student demand, questions of quality, and an explosion of new technologies are forcing colleges and universities up a steep learning curve. Concepts like privatization, decentralization, cost centers, ranking, and virtual learning—once anathemas to the academy—are ideas now being taken seriously by administrators and academic leaders—chancellors, provosts, deans, and department chairs.

But these stately organizations are not structured to chase opportunity like fast moving corporations. Nor do faculty members think like corporate employees. Instead, colleges and universities are loosely linked alliances of administrators and faculty members. Buttressed by traditions of academic freedom, these institutions were designed not to change easily with the times. So as the higher education environment becomes more turbulent, administrators and academic leaders are frequently caught between opposing forces that both demand change and at the same time resist it.

Predictions in Higher Education

Increasing Demand for Higher Education

All indications are that student demand for higher education is going to increase dramatically. For instance, in California it is being called "Tidal Wave II" in which a half million new students are predicted to enroll in higher education by 2006. Other states are also bracing for staggering surges in enrollments. Nationally, enrollments are projected to grow nearly 20%

through 2015, with 80% of the growth among African-American, Hispanic, and Asian students ("College campuses will grow," 2000). In a recent study, 77% of a national sample of parents report that a college education is more important than it was 10 years ago. Eighty-seven percent agree that a college education is as important as a high school diploma used to be (Measuring, 2000). And, African-American and Hispanic parents are especially confident that a college education is essential for their children's success.

Offsetting Reduced Subsidies

It is also becoming clear that higher education—particularly public universities that depend on direct subsidies—will not retain the high levels of state support as they have in the past. Escalating demands for prisons, K-12 education, and health and other services are outstripping an increasing number of states' total revenue. In all likelihood, higher education's share will continue to diminish as competition for scarce resources forces policy leaders to reduce higher education spending in the face of these other priorities (*Measuring*, 2000).

Raise tuition. One way to offset reduced public subsidies for operating costs and student aid is to raise tuition—a step that an increasingly large number of colleges and universities are taking. In many states, tuition continues to rise faster than either inflation or family income. Stanford economist Martin Anderson notes that between 1976 and 1996, the average annual tuition at public universities rose from $642 to $3,151. Private institutions' tuition rose from $2,881 to $15,581 (Francis, 2000). Increasingly, the difference between costs and families' ability to pay is born by students who are increasingly forced to borrow. And they are going deeply into debt. Says Terry Hartle, senior vice president of the American Council on Education, "It is not uncommon for a student to graduate with a bachelor's degree and $20,000 worth of debt. That would have been unheard of 15 to 20 years ago" (Brownstein, 2000). Elected officials know there is a limit to how much of these costs can be passed along to students and their families, leading a growing number of states like Ohio and California to cap tuition in public universities.

Cutting costs. Another way to offset lost revenue—something most academic administrators try to avoid—is cutting costs. Universities are complex institutions and cost cutting is not as straightforward as some may think. In fact, economist Anderson observes that college cost data are "indecipherable." "It's impossible to tell what's really going on...Universities are tricky places." Cornell labor economist Ronald Ehrenberg believes that administrators avoid cutting costs because universities avoid conflict, are risk aversive, and are slow to react when the environment changes. By the time administrators recognize the need to reduce costs, the crisis has passed (Ehrenberg, 2000).

M. Peter McPherson, president of Michigan State University, who served as Deputy Treasury Secretary under President Ronald Reagan, explained his frustration. Universities, McPherson says, "are filled with bright people with exceedingly good ideas." But, he adds, these bright people don't like to set priorities and the lack of priorities fosters unchecked spending. He elaborates, "I've run big government agencies and part of the Bank of America. There is more pressure to spend money on a college campus than any place I've ever worked" (Brownstein, 2000).

Nevertheless, a growing number of universities—especially private colleges that are less encumbered by state oversight—have read the environment accurately and are seriously trimming their budgets. According to David Warren, president of the National Association of Independent Colleges and Universities, more and more institutions of higher education are putting freezes on hiring and wage increases, eliminating weak programs and conserving energy. Others are taking more drastic action, contracting out services like cafeterias, campus security, computerization, and bookstores and reformulating programs.

Cutting costs in a university invariably leads to conflict. For instance at Michigan State, many of the faculty were up in arms when the administration made deep budget cuts, claiming that trimming budgets would only dampen the ability of the university to carry out its important social mission and translate into lower educational quality.

Other actions. On other campuses, harsh administrative action has been met with surprising reactions. For instance in 2000, University of Chicago President Hugo Sonnenschein's plans to brighten up the university's stodgy image and increase revenue led to his resignation. No sooner did he announce plans to reduce the number of core courses and expand the less costly undergraduate student body, than he was bitterly denounced by students and faculty. Faculty leaders accused Sonnenschein of undermining the university's strong intellectual traditions. And, at a "fun-in" to satirize Sonnenschein's plans that many feared would "dumb down" the curriculum, students improvised "The Great Books in One Minute" and announced the existence of "… an acute leadership crisis, primarily on the level of the president" (Gose, 1999; Bronner, 1999).

To avoid cost cutting and the inevitable conflict it produces has led some administrators to try to increase faculty productivity—an alternative that sometimes creates even worse results. For instance in 1997, the University of Florida began an experiment to see if it could boost faculty productivity in revenue producing areas of teaching, research, and fundraising through incentives. According to the plan, funds would be allocated to colleges based on faculty productivity and quality. While many administrators regard the idea as an unqualified success, it has many critics. One critic, H. Jane Brockmann, chair of the Department of Sociology at the University of Florida, said of the incentive plan:

> It is the wrong metaphor for higher education. We as a faculty do not measure our product in student credit, hours, graduation rates and so forth, because they don't measure what we really care about, which is how well-educated the students are and how much they have been professionalized. (Lively, 1999)

Other states are following Florida's lead. For instance, Virginia is now basing payments to campuses on increases in faculty productivity. In what many academics consider an assault on the academy, administrators at Boston University decided against using incentives and instead tried to force tenured professors to spend more time on campus, but without much success.

The evidence suggests that voluntary action may be insufficient to overcome campus resistance to reducing costs. There is a growing consensus that market competition will ultimately force changes that cannot be accomplished voluntarily. And competition is intensifying. The Christian Science Monitor reported:

> Alternative certifications, corporate education, and online for-profit universities are all gobbling market share from traditional colleges and universities. Competition is growing. Fast. (Clayton, 2001)

New Forces for Change

Accountability

Most colleges and universities are strangers in a competitive environment where institutions survive by carving out specialized market niches. In commercial markets, consumers differentiate products by their price and perceived value; in higher education, very little information is available to make a reasoned choice. Rarely do colleges and universities publish their completion and job placement rates. Rather, they prefer to distinguish themselves on the basis of reputation. In fact, they often react to the idea of this kind of disclosure with hostility.

Twenty-five years ago in a well-meaning gesture, the director of the University of Michigan's placement office compiled and published a list of all 1976-1977 graduates by their major field of study and their first jobs. A reader could not help but be struck by the huge number of graduates—especially those from the humanities and social sciences—who became taxi drivers, busboys, waiters, and graduate students. When the report became public it confirmed the worst suspicions of powerful conservative legislators—that public undergraduate education was little more than a training ground for graduate school. The placement director lost his job and the report was buried.

Now, a quarter of a century later, there is still a dearth of information about higher education outcomes. A recent study found that no states had information that describes the outcomes of their colleges and universities. Pat Callan, president of the National Center for Public Policy and Higher Education that issued the report, says:

> As an educator, it's an embarrassment that we can tell people almost anything about education except how well students are learning. (Abel, 2000)

Many educators claim that education is too complex to be measured so the void is filled by subjective rankings made each year by *U.S. News and World Report*. And, as we shall see later in this book, these rankings have a powerful impact on some academic units. Trying to assess the value of higher education is difficult because it is a complex process that has a range of outcomes. Perhaps lulled by a sense of complacency, many educators blindly resist the idea claiming that it leads to dumbing down the curriculum and trivializing education (Abel, 2000).

Virtual Education

High costs, lack of information on outcomes, and colleges' and universities' unresponsiveness makes them especially vulnerable to competition. Probably the greatest threat is virtual higher education, now made possible by new technology. "It is a $280 billion market, and it is an attractive one in which to compete," says Yale business school professor David Callis. He warns, "… the insurgents who will transform [higher education]… will be wolves in sheeps' clothing. The revolutionaries will be corporate America and in their van will be the Internet startups" (Callis, 2001).

And the revolutionaries are coming. Large for-profit corporations like Jones International University and the University of Phoenix have entered the huge and growing virtual university market to claim their share. A recent decision by a regional accrediting association, the historically conservative gatekeepers to higher education, has thrown the academy into a quandary. In 1999, the North Central Association shocked the educational establishment by approving Jones International University, an institution that provides its educational programs on the Internet. By all indications, Jones is just the beginning. Today, more than 60% of all American colleges and universities—including such noted universities as Carnegie Mellon, MIT, Duke, Harvard, and Stanford—offer educational programs online.

But many faculty leaders remain deeply skeptical. James Perley, a professor at the College of Wooster and chair of the American Association of University Professors Committee on Accreditation, is alarmed. He fears that the growing number of virtual universities will "destroy the tradition of higher education as a community of scholars defining 'what and who we are'." Michael Lambert, executive director of a private distance education group, dismisses this traditional faculty resistance as nothing more than self-protection, the fear of "an erosion of faculty freedom." The truth seems to be that no one knows where virtual education is going. David A. Longanecker, a former Assistant Secretary at the US Department of Education says, "It's leading us to a very different concept of quality assurance than we've traditionally had—but I'm not sure what that is" (Olson, 1999).

No matter what it turns out to be, indications are that virtual higher education will surely become a large enterprise. According to John Chambers, CEO of Cisco Systems, the company that makes routers that direct traffic on the Internet, education is the next big "killer application." Chambers believes that "Education over the Internet is going to be so big it is going to make email usage look like a rounding error!" Chambers warns, "Schools and countries that ignore this will suffer the same fate as big department stores that thought e-commerce was overrated" (Friedman, 1999).

And, because of its boundaryless quality, virtual higher education is an international phenomenon. Chambers explains. "Unlike in the industrial revolution when you had to be in the right country or city to participate, in this new era capital will flow to whichever countries and companies install the best Internet and educational capabilities." Chambers is certain that change cannot be held back. He says, "Governments and unions will be powerless to stop this capital flow, which will affect the global balance of economic power. It will take about ten years to be fully in place. But, it's coming next."

Privatization

Privatization too has become a global phenomenon in higher education. Just in 1999, students in Hungary, claiming that government imposed tuition would turn higher education into a market economy, turned back a new government policy to pass costs onto parents and students. Likewise, officials in countries such as Mexico, Ghana, Thailand, Australia, and China have been met with angry student reactions to government attempts to bail out cash-strapped public universities. Spurred by rising secondary graduation rates, student demand for university education is rising faster than public revenue to support it. Especially in nations like China and Thailand, hit by the Asian economic recession, steps to make universities more self-sufficient are met with vocal opposition (Woodward, 2000).

How to Change?

New forces for change—accountability, privatization, and virtual learning, to name just a few—have now arrived at higher education's doorstep. What to do about them is another matter. Administrators and academic leaders are increasingly perplexed about whether to make their universities more nimble to enable quick responses to external changes. Or should they embrace the time-tested academic form of organization? How much should universities respond to changes in student and employer demands? Should universities become more transparent to promote accountability and adaptation? Or should they retain the mysterious opaqueness that buffers them from changes and elevates their status?

These are the questions this book seeks to answer. We also hope to provide administrators and faculty leaders with new ways of thinking and communicating about this new environment. Without fresh and accurate concepts, and a language to express them, managing changes that are now sweeping across campuses will surely prove impossible.

The structure and culture of higher education have been geared toward its social mission as the chief agency entrusted with the preservation and transmission of existing knowledge and the generation of new knowledge. The university plays a key role in defining for society what counts as knowledge, so its ivory tower image is well suited to its need for opaqueness and mystique. Its departmental structure helps define boundaries of knowledge that enables disciplines to compete for continued legitimacy and survival. But how the core work of the university—research, teaching, and public service—is actually done is not at all well understood. If academic leaders are to help their institutions adapt to changing conditions, they must understand how this work is done.

Understanding Change

Classic Studies

Classic studies done in the 1970s and 1980s describe how universities operate as loosely coupled professional bureaucracies. Loosely coupled means that actions in one part of the organization need not be closely linked with another. For instance, in most research universities, philosophers and physicists have little more in common than a faculty club and a system of grading. Moreover, universities are professional bureaucracies. While faculty members operate with autonomy, their knowledge and routines have been standardized in their many years of training. Professional faculty members teach and conduct research in ways that conform to the standards of their fields. And, the university's core work processes are also specialized and standardized as are the processes by which students are selected into them.

The task for academic leaders is to somehow integrate these highly specialized units into a coherent organizational form. The result produces a constant tension between opposing requirements for differentiation and integration (Weick, 1976; Lawrence & Lorsch, 1967). Not surprisingly, as universities are faced with these competing demands, more and more administrators are required to manage increasing complexity at higher levels.

As the environment around higher education has become more complex and unpredictable, the academic vocabulary has been grudgingly expanded to include *restructuring, inputs* and *outputs, entrepreneurial leadership,* and *strategy.* At the same time, new body of research has begun to emerge under the general heading of adaptation or transformation. These newer bodies of work conceptualize organizations as open systems that seek to maintain equilibrium in a changing environment by managing exchanges across its boundaries (Pfeffer & Salancik, 1978; Cameron, 1984; Gumport & Pusser, 1999).

Most of this research provides useful descriptions but it offers little help to the hard-pressed administrator or faculty leader. For instance, contingency theory is used to help explain how universities integrate functions in times of rapid change that also demand specialization. The basic idea is that organizations are more adaptive when their core processes are properly aligned with other subsystems such as human resources and finance (Clark, 1993, 1995; Dill & Sporn, 1995). Population ecology represents yet another conception of how organizations adapt to changing conditions through natural selection by environmental requirements. According to population ecologists, organizational forms arise and survive in direct response to demands from the environment (Hannan & Freeman, 1977). Another view of how universities evolve is called organizational ecology. According to this perspective, universities are regarded as part of the environment, not separate from it, and survive best by avoiding conflict and by cooperating to coevolve. Yet another view of the adaptive university comes from the concept of "institutional isomorphism," which describes how organizations mimic each other as they adapt to help ensure their legitimacy and chances of survival (DiMaggio & Powell, 1983). Yet none of these ideas has been applied systematically to higher education, nor have they been particularly useful to the practitioner faced with balancing competing demands. (For a thoughtful review of this literature see Gumport & Sporn, 1999.)

Academic Decision-Making

Just how decisions are made in academic organizations has been debated for decades. In 1959, Yale University political economist Charles Lindblom expressed skepticism about rational planning in a messy human world and popularized the idea of nonrational planning or the "art of muddling through" as he called it (Lindblom, 1959). Later, Cohen, March, and Olsen developed the "garbage can" model of decision-making, which recognized chaotic conditions inherent in university decision-making, akin to "organized anarchy" (Cohen, March, & Olsen, 1972).

Other scholars argue that strategy is more than just pure chaos; it emerges through a rational, though nonlinear, process. In 1978, Quinn coined the term *logical incrementalism* to describe how patterns ultimately emerge from seemingly chaotic decision-making, enabling organizations to make purposeful but slow progress (Quinn, 1978). A few years later organizational theorist Henry Mintzberg observed, "… ironically, the overall strategic orientation of professional organizations seems to remain remarkably stable while individual strategies seem to be in a state of almost continual change" (Mintzberg, 1994).

Strategic Planning

One promising concept that has gained in stature since the environment began to change falls under the general rubric of strategic planning. It grew out of work in the private sector that aimed to help businesses understand their environments, define market niches, and use resources strategically to achieve goals and objectives. In a strategic planning framework, universities are considered coalitions of interest groups (Thompson, 1967; Cyert & March, 1992). Administrators play a central role by making "strategic choices" in the use of resources, following models of planning used in the corporate world that include scanning the environment, formulating and implementing strategies, evaluating the results, and making adjustments.

But strategic planning rarely works when it is applied to higher education. A former editor of *Planning in Higher Education* wrote in 1997:

> In the past dozen years, hundreds of the 3,500 colleges and universities in the United States have launched efforts at strategic planning... These hundreds of efforts have had mixed success. A few institutions have transformed themselves dramatically. Others have been able to make important changes in parts of their operation... But many institutions have stumbled, dissolved into controversy, or lost their nerve. (Rowley, Lujan, & Dolence, 1997)

Strategic planning often fails because colleges and universities are not corporations—though enthusiastic administrators often make the mistake of trying to draw a literal comparison between the two (Rowley, Lujan, & Dolence, 1997). They can be more accurately described as professional bureaucracies. They have all of the stability-assuring qualities that sociologist Max Weber described—hierarchical authority, specialization of labor, and general rules that when applied to individual cases make actions fair and predictable (Wilson, 1989); but they also depend on professional employees who have the power to establish their own conditions of work. While strategic plans may be made by university administrators, they cannot be implemented without the consent of the professional faculty who can (and do) veto unpopular plans (Birnbaum, 1991). To succeed in changing strategic direction, the faculty must be engaged in and committed to the planning process, which is difficult for reasons we will explore later.

Professional bureaucracies have an additional problem. Historically, universities have buffered faculty members from external pressures and uncertainty so they can carry out the core functions—teaching, research, and service—without external influence (Thompson, 1967). But buffering also has the unintended consequence of thwarting adaptation to a rapidly changing environment (Scott, 1998).

According to Mintzberg:

> Change in the professional bureaucracy does not sweep in from new administrators taking office to announce major reforms. Rather, change seeps in by the slow process of changing the professionals—changing who can enter the profession, what they learn in its professional skills (norms as well as skills and knowledge), and thereafter how willing they are to upgrade their skills. (Mintzberg & Quinn, 1998)

For these reasons, traditional strategic planning is not an easy fit with universities. Trying to force it, according to Mintzberg, is like "trying to fit the square pegs of planning into the round holes of [the university] organization." The misfit is summarized by one dean who said, "I see planning as an expanding bureaucracy, of very little assistance to me but capable of creating several structures of bullshit that I have to cope with" (Hardy, Langley, Mintzberg, & Rose, 1984).

Lack of a common conception or language. Administration-led attempts that use businesslike strategies that threaten to reallocate resources and power often set off howls of protest from faculty members. The tone of these conflicts reveals a deep divide in beliefs between administrators and faculty as well as a lack of a common language with which to communicate. For instance, James Carlin, a businessman who recently stepped down as chair of the Massachusetts Board of Higher Education, angered academics when he announced:

> Colleges and universities, in general, are grossly inefficient and ineffective in terms of how they manage their enterprises... But if somebody makes a suggestion that maybe you shouldn't have four Egyptian history professors on a campus where only ten kids are majoring in Egyptian history—and maybe you ought to let three of those professors go—you've got a [faculty] revolution on your hands... You've got underutilization of the physical plant—you've got tenure—which basically ties your hands on how you can manage your work force... (Clayton, 1999)

We had a preview of just how wide this divide really is at a recent meeting of the Social Science Research Council. There we previewed ideas contained in this book with a group of scholars who study organizational change in higher education. Once concepts like core processes, inputs, outputs, performance measures, and outcomes entered the conversation, friendly deliberation turned hostile. Our attempt to describe the use of an open systems framework was quickly interpreted as imposing an industrial model on higher education. We were accused of making the university dangerously transparent and of measuring things that could be used against faculty members by budget-cutting administrators.

This conversation signaled the need to find a new way to help administrators and academic leaders learn from America's industrial experience and to communicate about it. After all, many corporations and unions have already learned how to accurately read and adjust to changes in the environment. By telling how one large research university responded to its environment, we hope to open a wider conversation without producing a defensive reaction.

There is much to be learned from a close examination of industry, though one must be artful with interpretation because of vast differences between these two kinds of institutions. We have spent a decade studying how corporations and unions strain to survive under the forces of change and how some have emerged as healthy and productive organizations (Wilms, 1996; Zell, 1997). From studies of New United Motor Manufacturing, Inc. (NUMMI), the GM-Toyota joint venture; USS-POSCO, the joint venture between the Korean steelmaker POSCO and America's USS; the now defunct Douglas Aircraft, and electronics giant Hewlett-Packard (HP), we witnessed the difficulty of this kind of adaptation even in the corporate sector. Changes that enabled some companies to survive and prosper required radical alterations of organizational structure and belief that could emerge only under galvanic pressure. For instance, that American autoworkers and executives would one day accept a Japanese production system that requires employee participation and interdependence was at one time unthinkable. Similarly, the idea that HP engineers could break through a paralyzing culture of complacency and learn to design products demanded by their customers required a giant step into the unknown.

While strategies used by these companies do not obviously translate directly to higher education, they offer analogies and some fresh ways of thinking about the university. For instance, we learned how altering an organization's core work processes, whether building automobiles or airplanes, making steel, or designing and building high tech electronics, shapes its culture, not the other way around. To change an organization's culture, we saw how the core work processes could be redesigned to require broad participation by employees up and down the chain of command.

Plan of the Book

This book is intended to help administrators and academic leaders think differently about their institutions and be better prepared to guide them in a fast moving environment. What follows is a detailed account of a large research university that is struggling to adapt to external pressures that are forcing changes within.

We headed a team of graduate students who for three years dug deeply into the University of California Los Angeles (UCLA). The research team was positioned in three key units of the university—the Anderson School (business), the Graduate School of Education and Information Studies, and the Department of Physics and Astronomy. These three units—two professional schools and two core disciplines—gave us varied viewpoints on how the university interacts with its environment and how it manages its own processes of change.

Trying to understand the university's relationship to its external environment led to the choice of open systems theory to frame the study. Open systems theory—a concept that derives from biology—emerged in the 1960s in response to the static nature of earlier research frameworks. Until the 1960s when steady growth characterized the environment in which most organizations operated, they were usually characterized as "closed systems" that could operate successfully without feedback from the environment (Scott, 1998; Thompson, 1967). In contrast, an open system is one that exists in constant exchange with its environment; this system has one or more feedback loops that provide the entity with information from the environment that allows it to alter its processes while in progress. Inputs from the environment cross the boundary into the system where they are transformed by processes into outputs that leave the system's boundaries. These outputs are consumed directly by customers and are of benefit indirectly to stakeholders and the society at large. While earlier frameworks either ignored organizations' environments or viewed them as alien or hostile, an open systems perspective considers the environment to be the ultimate source of materials, energy, and information, all of which are vital to the continuation of the system (Scott, 1998). If sealed off from their environments, or lacking feedback loops, according to open systems theory, organizations will ultimately die. The open system is shown in Figure 1.1.

An open systems framework is easily applied to a university. The university creates outputs that affect, and/or are used by, the outside environment. At the same time, the university draws on the environment for inputs. The university is not simply passive in this exchange. Changes and stresses in the environment occurring for reasons external to the university, may create demands and constraints that affect the university. Similarly, the outputs from the university may have significant effects for the outside environment that cause it to react in ways that again affect the university. In addition to the major feedback loop from outputs, to the environment, to inputs, there may be feedback loops that act between the outputs and internal university processes, or between the university and its inputs.

For instance, universities import resources, including undergraduate and graduate students, new faculty and staff, and financial resources. They also seek to generate and maintain broader social and political support for their activities, support which in turn can be translated into financial and other resources and independence of action. They engage in educational processes that convert incoming students into exportable graduates, personnel practices in which some new professors

Figure 1.1 *The University as an Open System*

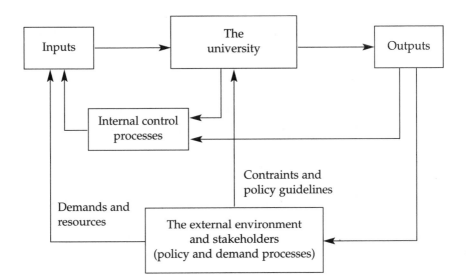

are converted into tenured faculty, and research activities that produce knowledge of varying degrees of abstraction and immediate practical utility.

Universities then export graduates with degrees who are employed by the private and public sector economies. Other universities are employers of many students who earn PhDs. In addition to graduates, universities also export published research findings that are consumed both by the private and public sectors, and by other universities. Finally, they engage in a broad range of consultative activities that translate research into forms of knowledge that can be readily consumed by private and public sector organizations.

We wanted to find out the nature of UCLA's external environment and how the university responds to it. We also wanted to know how outputs of the university are evaluated by key stakeholders. Within the three units, we wanted to find out how the cultures of each differed and the implications for how they interact with the larger environment, use resources, and configure their core processes. We hoped to discover how the core work processes—research, teaching, and service—are carried out. Finally, we hoped to discover how broad external forces are interpreted at the unit level, how adjustments are made, and the consequences.

We used a variety of research methods to delve into life in these units over a time period that extended from 1996 to 2000. Our methods included participant observation, interviews, mapping core work processes and social networks, time use analysis, and financial analysis. (For a detailed discussion of these methods and their application in a university setting, please visit our web site at www.gseis.ucla.edu/faculty/pages/Wilms.html.)

Chapter Two describes UCLA and its larger environment, which is especially important to a multicampus university. Chapters Three–Five describe each of the three academic units, their cultures and core processes, and how they adapted to external pressures. Chapter Six draws the key findings together in a discussion aimed to help administrators and academic leaders understand their environments and mobilize the faculty to help move in a coordinated direction.

Let us now turn to the story of UCLA and the broader implications of its experience.

References

Abel, D. (2000, December 28). Measuring what college students learn proves elusive. *The Boston Globe*, p. 1.

Birnbaum, R. (1991). The latent organization functions of the academic senate: Why senates do not work but will not go away. In R. Birnbaum (Ed.), *Faculty in governance: The role of senates and joint committees in academic decision making*. New Directions for Higher Education, No. 75. San Francisco, CA: Jossey-Bass.

Bronner, E. (1999, June 5). U of Chicago president to return to teaching. *New York Times*, p. A10.

Brownstein, A. (2000, October 27). Tuition rises faster than inflation, and faster than in previous year. *The Chronicle of Higher Education*, p. A50.

Callis, D. (2001). *Storming the ivory tower*. Unpublished paper, Harvard Business School, Cambridge, MA.

Cameron, K. (1984). Organizational adaptation and higher education. *Journal of Higher Education*, 55 (2), 122-144.

Clark, B. R. (1995). Complexity and differentiation: The deepening problem of integration. In D. D. Dill and B. Sporn (Eds.), *Emerging patterns of social demand and university reform: Through a glass darkly*. Oxford, England: Pergamon.

Clark, B. (1993). *The higher education system: Academic organization in cross-national perspective*. Berkeley, CA: University of California Press.

Clayton, M. (2001, January 2). Higher education's undercurrents. *The Christian Science Monitor*, p. 10.

Clayton, M. (1999, June 29). Taking on 'sacred cows' in higher education. *The Christian Science Monitor*, p. 18.

Cohen, M. D., & March, J. G. (1976). Decisions, presidents, and status. In J. G. March & J. P. Olsen (Eds.), *Ambiguity and choice in organizations.* Bergen, Norway: Universitetsforlaget.

Cohen, M. D., March, J. G., & Olsten, J. P. (1972). A garbage can model of organizational choice. *Administrative Science Quarterly, 17*, 1-25.

College campuses will grow more diverse, report says. (2000, June 2). *The Chronicle of Higher Education*, p. A51.

Cyert, R., & March, J. G. (1992). *A behavioral theory of the firm* (2nd ed.). Englewood Cliffs, NJ: Prentice Hall.

Dill, D. D., & Sporn, B. (1995). University 2001: What will the university of the twenty-first century look like? In D. D. Dill & B. Sporn (Eds.), *Emerging patterns of social demand and university reform: Through a glass darkly.* Oxford: Pergamon.

DiMaggio, P. J., & Powell, W. W. (1983). The iron cage revisited: Institutional isomorphism and collective rationality in organizational fields. *American Sociological Review, 48*, 147-160.

Ehrenberg, R. (2000). *Why college costs so much.* Boston, MA: Harvard University Press.

Francis, D. (2000, January 18). Step right up for some higher education about the real costs of college. *The Christian Science Monitior*, p. 17.

Friedman, T. (1999, November 17). Foreign affairs: Next it's education. *The New York Times*, p. A25.

Gose, B. (1999, June 18). A president's controversial legacy. *The Chronicle of Higher Education*, p. A43.

Gumport, P., & Pusser, B. (1999). University restructuring: The role of economic and political contexts. In J. Smart & W. Tierney (Eds.), *Higher education: Handbook of theory and research, XIV.* New York, NY: Agathon.

Gumport, P. J., & Sporn, B. (1999). Institutional adaptation: Demands for management reform and university administration. In J. Smart & W. Tierney (Eds.), *Higher education: Handbook of theory and research, XIV*. New York, NY: Agathon.

Hannan, M., & Freeman, J. (1997). The population ecology of organization. *American Journal of Sociology*, 82 (5), 929-964.

Hardy, C., Langley, A., Mintzberg, H., & Rose, J. (1984). Strategy formation in the university setting. In J. Bess (Ed.), *College and university organization: Insights for the behavioral sciences*. New York, NY: New York University Press.

Lawrence, P., & Lorsch, J. (1967). Differentiation and integration in complex organizations. *Administrative Science Quarterly*. 12:1-47.

Lindblom, E. (1959, Spring). The science of muddling through. *Public Administration Review*, 79-88.

Lively, K. (1999, February 26). U. of Florida's 'bank' rewards colleges that meet key goals. *The Chronicle of Higher Education*, p. A35.

Measuring Up 2000 (2000, November 30). National Center for public policy and higher education. San Jose, CA.

Mintzberg, H. (1994). *The rise and fall of strategic planning*. New York, NY: Free Press.

Mintzberg, H., & Quinn, J. (1998). *Readings in the strategy process* (3rd ed.). Englewood Cliffs, NJ: Prentice Hall.

Olson, F. (1999, August 6). Virtual institutions challenge accreditors to devise new ways of measuring quality. *The Chronicle of Higher Education*, p. A29.

Pfeffer, J., & Salancik, G. (1978). *The external control of organizations: A resource dependence perspective*. New York, NY: Harper & Row.

Quinn, J. B. (1978). *Strategies for change: Logical incrementalism*. Homewood, IL: Richard D. Irwin, Inc.

Rowley, D., Lujan, H., & Dolence, M. (1997). *Strategic change in colleges and universities*. San Francisco, CA: Jossey-Bass.

Scott, W. R. (1998). *Organizations: Rational, natural, and open systems*. Upper Saddle River, NJ: Prentice Hall.

Thompson, J. D. (1967). *Organizations in action*. New York, NY: McGraw Hill.

Weick, K. (1976, March). Educational organizations as loosely coupled systems. *Administrative Science Quarterly*.

Wilms, W. W. (1996). *Restoring prosperity: How workers and managers are forging a new culture of cooperation*. New York, NY: Random House.

Wilson, J. Q. (1989). *Bureaucracy*. New York, NY: Basic Books.

Woodward, C. (2000, May 5). Worldwide tuition increases send students into the streets. *The Chronicle of Higher Education*, p. A54.

Zell, D. M. (1997). *Changing by design: Work innovation at Hewlett-Packard*. New York, NY: Cornell Press.

2

UCLA and Its Larger Environment

Along with the University of California-Berkeley, UCLA is considered California's premier public university. With thousands more students hoping to attend each year than there are seats to hold them, UCLA has its choice of California's college-going students. Located in one of the most dynamic and trend-setting megacities, UCLA is rated consistently among the top research universities in the world. It has earned this distinction in a relatively short period of time—a little more than 80 years.

UCLA began in 1882 as a teacher's college—California's second State Normal School. It first was located on the downtown site that today is the Central Los Angeles Public Library. To accommodate the growing student demand, it moved in 1914 to what is now Los Angeles City College near Hollywood. In 1919, the Normal School became the Southern Branch of the University of California, then consisting only of the Berkeley campus in Northern California. UCLA's first class graduated in 1925. The name "University of California at Los Angeles," and ground breaking for the Westwood campus came two years later.

Today, the park-like campus on LA's Westside contains nearly 300 buildings on more than 400 acres of land. It has its own post office, police department, museums, theaters, student-run stores and restaurants, and a large athletic arena. On an average day, more than 60,000 people traverse the campus to take classes, work in offices and laboratories, teach in classrooms, visit art galleries, or see doctors at the large medical complex. Fourteen libraries that contain 7.1 million volumes dot the campus and its neighboring community. The university library consistently ranks among the top four research libraries in North America.

UCLA enrolls the most ethnically mixed and culturally diverse undergraduate student population—both in total students and as percentage of enrollment—of any major university in the United States. Ethnic minorities comprise 62% of the undergraduates and 42% of the graduate students. Most students are Californians, but the student population includes representation from all 50 states and more than 115 foreign countries. The average freshman enters with a 4.08 grade point average (this is possible with advance placement and college prep course credit) and average Scholastic Assessment Test (SAT) scores of 1275. The average age of undergraduates is 21, and the average graduate student is 29.

UCLA provides a broad range of academic offerings through 12 academic units. The College of Letters and Science that houses the core disciplines is the center of undergraduate education. In addition, UCLA has 11 professional schools—the largest number of professional schools of any single University of California campus—including medicine, law, management, engineering, arts and architecture, theater, film and television, and education and information studies.

UCLA's 35,550 students are enrolled in 116 undergraduate degree programs, 86 master's programs, and 108 doctoral and professional degree programs. Approximately 9,500 degrees are awarded each year.

Students are taught by approximately 1,500 regular rank teaching faculty (called "ladder" faculty) and another 470 who are lecturers or other teaching faculty. Though not representative of its diverse student population, UCLA's faculty is more ethnically diverse than most other research universities.

UCLA Extension, the largest urban-based continuing higher-education program in the country, employs another 764 teachers. Extension offers more than 4,500 courses a year on campus, at satellite centers, and online.

UCLA is part of the 170,000-student, nine-campus University of California (UC) system, which is about to add a tenth campus. The system, which was established as a land-grant university, is governed by a governor-appointed Board of

Regents. The California Master Plan of Higher Education differentiates UC's role from that of the California State University's 23 campuses and the 103 community colleges, as doctoral training and research.

While all UC campuses follow certain system-wide policies, such as student admissions procedures and faculty promotions, the remainder of this chapter will illustrate how UCLA and its sister campuses also act independently of and in some cases competitively with each other as they maneuver through their external environments. As we shall see, the way in which a campus adapts to changes creates other change farther down the line in the professional schools and departments.

UCLA as Part of a Larger System

As we discussed earlier, we conceived of UCLA as an open system—an organization with permeable boundaries that is in constant exchange with its environment. We also knew that certain organizations in the environment—though when we began this book we were unclear just which ones they were—depend on UCLA and feel they have a stake in its success. These stakeholders in turn can have a powerful impact on the university's resources. Reasoning that exchanges with stakeholders can have an important impact on the university's internal operations, we wanted to find out how it manages these exchanges and manages its boundaries in a time of change.

It quickly became clear that the organizational environment encompassing UCLA is varied and complex, similar to environments surrounding most large, formal, public organizations. There are many different agencies, some of which have formal ties to the university, while some have only informal connections. Some maintain continual relationships with the university, while some have cyclical, and others episodic relationships. But one thing was unmistakable—UCLA's environment is growing increasingly complex, particularly when it comes to issues of public funding and new sources of revenue.

Like any multicampus university, UCLA does not act independently. The larger UC system, with its own bureaucratic structure and decision-making apparatus, has a significant impact on campus-level decision-making. Not surprisingly, the individual campuses have interests and agendas that often conflict with one another. The system-wide administration exists in part to maintain order and resolve conflict, especially during the annual budget cycle when system-wide administrators also set campus enrollment figures that affect budget allocations. In earlier times when budget resources flowed more freely, conflict among the nine UC campuses was relatively minimal. However, in today's environment of constrained resources, the potential for conflict has increased. While for decades, UCLA competed only with UC Berkeley for resources, today it is being seriously challenged by several other UC campuses.

The UC operates within the state with a good deal of autonomy because it has its own constitution. Because of this constitutional independence, it has insulated itself more successfully from political demands than have many other comparable public universities such as the Universities of Illinois and Ohio. However, it is not invulnerable to political pressures, which often are applied during annual negotiations with the governor and state legislature. Political influences also are transmitted through powerful constituent groups and individuals who sometimes try to influence internal operations, especially student admissions and the academic program.

At the campus level, multiple stakeholders that depend on UCLA's output—especially employers and other agencies that use its graduates and products of its research—affect its internal academic units. And, as we shall see, within UCLA's own internal structure, the academic units act as though they are largely independent of one another, because of different cultures and processes and unique exchanges with their environments. Even within single academic units there can be wide variation in goals, internal processes, and ways of conducting business with other organizations. In this way, UCLA may more closely resemble a holding company of disparate entities that produce a variety of products and services, than a homogeneous university.

Exchanges with the Environment

UCLA imports various resources from its larger environments (undergraduate and graduate students, new faculty and staff, and financial resources) and then transforms these resources through internal processes into outputs (credentialled graduates, new professors, expert advice, consulting, and research products). In turn the outputs are exported back into their environments where they are evaluated. Positive evaluations generate and maintain broad social and political support that can be translated into budget dollars (and other resources) and independence of action.

These are the core activities of large public research universities like UCLA. In addition, there are a variety of other activities that they undertake in order to be able to perform these core activities.

Buffers

Because of the fact that organizations live in increasingly uncertain and uncontrollable environments, most prefer to operate as if they were closed systems to safeguard at least the illusion of certainty and to promote efficiency. One way they maintain stability in the face of changing external events is by constructing and maintaining buffer mechanisms that help protect the technical core from external influence—where the teaching, research and service are produced—by managing their boundaries and balancing input and output transactions. Some examples include student admissions and placement, alumni relations, public information, government relations and legal affairs, development, and business services.

In relatively quiescent environments where resources are plentiful, threats are low, and demand for organizational outputs are adequate, buffers occupy a position of lesser importance compared with core activities. However, when environments become turbulent, buffering functions ascend in importance because they buy the organization time to adjust internal processes to changing environmental conditions.

What follows are results of an investigation of a small but significant part of UCLA's external environment. We thought about how each of the three academic units might perceive its environment, including key stakeholders who depend on UCLA but who can also influence the flow of resources. Next, we checked these ideas with the deans of each of the three units under study and with people who work in these buffering functions. We interviewed a small but representative sample (about 40 individuals) to find out what they thought.

UCLA's Larger Environment

Four key events appear to have significantly altered UCLA's relationship to its larger environment.

1) **The fiscal picture:** The mix of funds UCLA receives has shifted dramatically during the past three decades. In 1966, somewhat less than half (44%) of all UCLA resources came from the state. Today, that percentage has slipped to 20%, with private funds rising from less than a quarter (23%) of all UCLA resources in 1966 to more than two-thirds (67%) today.

2) **Demographic changes:** There also has been a significant shift in California's population, with ethnic minorities now comprising the majority. In 1970, whites represented 77% of the population but by 2000 the percentage had fallen to less than 50%. Hispanics represent the fastest growing segment of the population and by 2021 they are expected to become California's largest ethnic group.

3) **The end of affirmative action:** In 1996 California voters passed Proposition 209, which outlawed affirmative action plans. As a result, UC campuses are under increased pressure to find alternative ways to recruit and retain under-represented students to ensure representative, ethnically diverse, student bodies.

4) **Term limits:** In 1990 California voters passed Proposition 140, which placed term limits on state legislators. The effects are now being felt as leadership roles in the

state Senate and Assembly are assumed by new legislators and especially increasing proportions of Hispanic lawmakers. Between 1990 and 1994 the population of the Latino Legislative Caucus doubled in size.

Because of the huge number of actors we could have discussed, we have selected two significant ones found within UCLA's larger environment: The state of California and the University of California system. Decisions made by agencies of the state and the University of California's Office of the President (UCOP) have a large influence on UCLA from the chancellor down to department chairs. What follows is a limited description of these two influences and how UCLA has responded to them.

State-wide Influences

From the state, we have selected two state government offices that in particular have a significant impact on the UC and UCLA. While such a limited sample is not intended to represent the totality of the relationship between the state and the university, even this limited examination reveals important dynamics of how UCLA reacts and adjusts to changes in its environment.

Legislative Analyst Office

The Legislative Analyst Office was established by joint rules of the California Senate and Assembly in 1941 to provide the legislature with an independent analysis of the annual budget. It conducts specialized analytic studies as well. As independent naysayer and critic, the legislative analyst often conflicts with the public agencies over which it wields influence. Because of its role, it tends to complicate the University of California's efforts to build close relationships with legislators and the governor. A UC official notes, "They are designed to create friction." He continued:

> They come out with outlandish critiques on things we are trying to do, and then we have to

> invest huge amounts of effort in rebutting all that
> stuff, and generally we succeed, but... it's just a
> huge drain. Like, for example, this year they
> came out with their own notion of what they
> think our capital budget should look like. They
> came up with some set of categories, first seismic
> and then enrollment or something. Well, if you
> apply that, the University of California would
> probably spend every nickel we could on seismic
> safety and have nothing left for enrollment
> growth (or) research facilities.

In better years, the governor's office tended to spread resources among the community colleges, the California State University system, and the University of California. But in leaner years, as budget demands have outstripped available resources, the importance of the Legislative Analyst's function has increased. And the fact of term limits on legislators will only add to the Legislative Analyst's importance as the legislature's institutional memory is diminished by rapid turnover.

Senate Office of Research

Another powerful state agency, the Senate Office of Research (SOR) provides legislators with policy research to inform legislative initiatives. While the Senate Office of Research conducts much of its own research, it also depends on the University of California. According to a Senate Office of Research official, UCLA and UC Berkeley are important because of a significant number of faculty members who have political experience who understand Sacramento (the state capital). "These faculty members have also shown a lot of willingness and interest in doing policy research for the Senate," she said.

Like the Legislative Analyst's Office, the Senate Office of Research's significance has grown since the passage of Proposition 140, which, in addition to establishing legislative term limits, also cut the legislature's operating budget by 40%. The effect was to reduce the size of the Senate's committee staffs and their ability to establish policy to guide legislation.

While the Senate Office of Research has established productive relationships with individual faculty members at UCLA and UC Berkeley, there has been a longstanding tension between the legislature and the University of California over the usefulness and relevance of much of the research produced by the university for policy. These tensions became visible in the early 1970s when the chair of Assembly higher education committee threatened to divert a large sum of money earmarked for the university to establish a new research enterprise that would be governed by the legislature. The resulting uproar eventually subsided with the university and the legislature devising a compromise to establish a policy research function within the university.

In a classic case of buffering UC's technical core, the California Policy Research Center was created to provide policy-relevant research. It has no faculty of its own, but serves as a coordinating point where faculty members can find financial support for their ideas, so long as they advance state policy. The center is governed by a steering committee appointed by the governor's office, the Senate and the Assembly, and the university. Now in its 15th year of operation, it has helped establish productive relationships between the legislature and the university by exchanging resources for policy-relevant research.

However, relationships between the two are often strained. Tensions stem in part from the university's broad mission to conduct basic, applied, and policy research, and from its constitutional independence that encourages a certain political aloofness from the fray in Sacramento. The university also is perceived as distant and unapproachable because of its stature as a top-tier, selective public university. Not surprisingly, policymakers sometimes criticize the university as being elitist and arrogant. One legislative staff member explained:

> In a recent education roundtable with Congressional committee members, the university representatives failed to mention students even once, never mentioned public service. It creates its own problems for itself by its conduct. Then it hides

behind this arrogance with testimonials about commitment to quality.

Some of the perception of the university being out of touch probably also stems from its centralized governance structure. Sitting atop the nine-campus system is the office of the president through which many significant transactions—including budgets—must be conducted. An SOR staff member said:

> It's hard to do business with individual campuses without the office of the president buying into it. We can do all the back-channeling we want, but when the UC people sit down with the governor's people to decide which of our little additions are going to stay and which are going to go, that's when the rubber meets the road. If you haven't cut a deal with the office of the president, you're done.

University of California
Office of the President (UCOP)

Now our discussion leads into the university itself where policy directives are made by a 26-member board of regents who are appointed by the governor and approved by the senate for 12-year terms. The regents in turn hire a president who is headquartered in Oakland. Since 1995, a former chancellor of the UC San Diego campus has served as president. While much of what goes on in Oakland may seem distant to faculty members at UCLA, its activities have a direct bearing on campus life. We now turn to some of the important functions of the office of the president.

UC Office of Governmental Relations

The office of governmental relations, headquartered in Sacramento, is the UCOP's eyes and ears in state government, where it monitors pending legislation that may affect the university. The office also formulates ideas for legislation and lobbies support from state officials and other interest groups. Much of its effort goes toward maintaining broad support for a single, consolidated budget for the entire UC system. This strategy is intended to minimize conflict between the campuses and the office of the president, because budgets do not result from specific allocations for each campus. Consequently there are few incentives for campuses to lobby against each other in the legislative process. As long as faculty members work within this structure, conflict and competition can be avoided. "The office of the president has to use a heavy hand sometimes," according to one UC official. "Collectively we can help to grow the budget for all campuses. If we start to stray off the reservation, there is the potential to damage our overall appropriation."

While coordination helps to reduce conflict among campuses, centralized control produces tension between the campuses and the office of the president. A campus-level official explained:

> I have to be attentive to people here on campus if I am going to be successful. To the extent that they have needs and desires outside of what the office of the president has deemed to be the priorities of the university, I have to figure out a way to work with them and not violate the sanctity of the system-wide prerogative. I spend a lot of time skirting that line, trying to be helpful to faculty and administrators at the campus and at the same time trying to keep them in line... It's a pretty fine line.

Not surprisingly, aggressive and independent faculty members from the campuses sometimes ignore the office of the president and lobby powerful legislators for their own projects outside of the formal planning and budgeting process. One official estimates that 2% to 4% of the university's total annual budget represents projects that emanate from outside the formal process. These end-runs can be problematic for campus administrators. A UCLA official described the tension that results:

I get calls from the office of the president and am
told, 'Somebody from UCLA is doing this or that,
and it's not consistent with what we want to see
happen. What are you going to do about it?'

Sometimes, attempts at end-runs are headed off at the campus level when senior administrators feel they have to step in.
In other cases, explained a UCLA official, they succeed.
"Sometimes you get these hard-headed faculty members who
say 'I don't give a damn what the office of the president thinks,
this is what I need for my center to thrive' and it costs us at
budget time."

Recently, as the proportion of the UC budget supported by
state money has declined, and as term limits have accelerated
turnover among legislators, the office of the president has
begun to reverse course and to encourage the campuses to work
more actively with legislators. One UC official explained, "Term
limits makes it more important than keeping order. It's a new
educational job to get new legislators up to speed quickly on the
university's problems."

Planning and Budgeting

Within the system-wide office, a planning and analysis unit
engages in long-term planning for student enrollment (from
three to five years into the future) for individual campuses and
the system as a whole. Enrollment planning drives both
instructional budgets and admissions processes at individual
campuses.

Enrollment planning depends heavily on high school graduation rates and trends identified by the State Department of
Finance. These figures are used to help individual campuses
plan for future enrollments within existing capital constraints.
Analysts from the system-wide planning office coordinate with
campus budget analysts, providing support for the annual
budget cycle. This relationship has been facilitated by a relatively stable staff, who have developed extensive informal
relationships.

Senior administrators from the nine campuses meet monthly to work on common problems and to develop an agenda for system-wide planning, including productivity improvements, budget pressures, and year-round campus operations to make three-year degrees a possibility. A council of chancellors also meets regularly to share information and to coordinate enrollment planning. These internal planning and analysis functions remain largely insulated from political pressures.

UCOP planners and analysts work primarily with legislative staff members and the California Post-Secondary Education Commission, a body that coordinates California's three-tiered postsecondary system. Planners say they have found the commission useful for working through issues such as student fees and student financial aid because it can coordinate with the California State University system. While the commission does not have any direct control over the UC, it is always seeking a more influential role. Not surprisingly, university officials have resisted any inroads on their independence, which they vigorously protect.

In 1995 the UC president began reworking the system used to allocate funds to the campuses. The result was a new budget initiative that emerged a year later in 1996. He was convinced that limited state support was a permanent condition that was not going to improve. He knew that 85% of California's budget is fixed, being statutorily protected. Whatever the university's share, it would come from the remaining 15% in open competition with K-12 education, the California community colleges, the 23 campus California State University system, and the rapidly growing prison system. The UC president recognized that the university would be compelled to manage its resources in new ways to maintain quality and meet increasing enrollment demands.

The UC budget initiative aimed to decentralize much of the planning and budgeting, leaving decision-making to the individual campuses—loosening up some of the strings—while holding chancellors accountable for meeting campus priorities including educational quality.

At about the same time, California's governor issued a higher education compact to help stabilize public support for higher education. This new agreement promised to increase the UC's operating budget by 4% each year in the form of a block grant, leaving it discretion as to how to spend it. The compact would also provide funds for debt service on revenue bonds and $150 million each year for capital expenditures.

Changes in the UC's planning and budgeting process followed the same block grant approach. Beginning in 1996, much of the budgeting authority (with some exceptions, like staff and faculty salary range adjustments) was passed down to the campus chancellors. In 1996, the budget and planning process was decentralized, giving individual campus chancellors more power over their financial destinies.

Early in the annual budget cycle, officials from the office of the president visit each campus and hold budget hearings to discuss changes like increases in undergraduate enrollments or new research initiatives that have budget implications. After UCOP officials arrive at a tentative budget, negotiations begin with the state Department of Finance, the Legislative Analyst Office, legislative committee consultants, and the governor. Simultaneous communications proceed between various levels of the UCOP staff and their counterparts in state government. The strategy is for UC to get as much of its budget as possible embedded in the governor's budget. As a result, there is an incentive to resolve as many issues as possible at the Department of Finance level. Finally, these negotiations culminate in a meeting between the governor and the UC president.

UCLA Buffering Functions

As previously mentioned, in turbulent times, organizations tend to elevate the importance of their buffering functions—operations that deal directly with the external environment—to buy time in order to adjust their processes. As our discussion returns to UCLA, we can see how this is true at the campus level.

UCLA Office of Government and Community Relations

One of the significant campus functions that enables UCLA to communicate with its larger environment is the office of government and community relations, which has grown in importance. An assistant vice chancellor explained:

> The university understood that the world is changing, both in terms of where it gets its money and how it is viewed externally. There's a need to be more proactive, more aggressive— aggressive in a nice way in terms of building relationships with elected officials and community officials that are important to the university.

UCLA's government relations office oversees and promotes federal, state, local government, and community relations. Although some academic units, especially the professional schools, have developed their own relationships with external groups, the central government relations office is the primary clearinghouse for UCLA's political relationships. The office serves a classic buffering function—coordinating activities across the campus and connecting external groups with internal university functions. One government relations official amplified:

> While we're helping steer the campus in their relationships with external groups, we're also helping those groups navigate their way on campus. UCLA can be a perplexing place for people who work here as well as people who don't. Part of my job is to help them define who to talk to and to engage the faculty, administrators, staff, and students.

UCLA's government relations office maintains contact with federal agencies, but depends heavily upon the UC office of the president, which maintains a Washington office, and upon higher education associations that lobby on its behalf. Most of its efforts focus on state-level officials. When issues arise that require face-to-face meetings between campus leaders and members of the legislature or the governor's staff, the office of government and community relations often plays a facilitating role. For instance, when legislators are first elected, the office often facilitates meetings with UCLA administrators and faculty members whose expertise may be useful to new lawmakers.

Planning and Budgeting

Mirroring economic changes in the larger environment, UCLA suffered budget reductions totaling more than $150 million between 1991 and 1994. Such deep operating budget cuts were all but unprecedented in the university's 75-year history. Except for temporary downturns, resources had grown steadily each year since 1975, and by 1990 UCLA's annual budget was $1.8 billion.

Until 1997, UCLA produced only one financial statement annually, and it was usually available five months after the fact. Because there was no system of feedback, the university was flying blind, unable to make decisions—a condition that was particularly risky in times of fiscal uncertainty and scarcity. Prior to 1997, the budget process focused on $35 million to $40 million in discretionary funds, which represented only 2% of UCLA's total budget. The remaining 98% was not considered. There was also a state fund mentality among budget planners, who routinely swept unused funds back into a central pool, leaving no incentives to reduce costs.

The chancellor at the time, who had held his position for nearly 30 years, was said to be the only person who understood the university's budget. Much of the budget's complexity stemmed from a wide range of accounting practices used across the campus and a vast array of cross subsidies. Consequently, it was very hard to accurately assess the cost of any given activity and to know where all the money was going. Until 1997 UCLA never had a fully reconcilable budget.

This chancellor reportedly knew UCLA's budget history by heart. He acknowledged that not much was known about the sources and uses of funds and of costs of space and administration, and explained:

The true resource flows within the university are obscured, and our ability to make fully informed resource allocations is weakened accordingly. We lack well-defined incentives for academic entrepreneurship (or resources development) and for banking resources for planned future investment. Our financial information system does not adequately support dynamic financial management, or make accountability for fiscal performance clear.

The philosophy of Responsibility Center Management. In 1994, the chancellor and his staff began to push information on costs and revenues down to individual academic and administrative units where deans would now have sufficient information and authority to make choices. UCLA's model drew heavily on the philosophy of Responsibility Center Management (RCM) that was undergoing trials at Indiana University, the University of Southern California, the University of Michigan, the University of Pennsylvania, and others (Whalen, 1991). For two years—between 1994 and 1996, groups of administrators benchmarked UCLA against other universities, while other groups, led by external consultants, analyzed how to implement this fiscal decentralization. Three academic units (largely the same ones selected for this book) were chosen as simulation sites to test how RCM might actually work in practice.

Changes were barely perceived as RCM was introduced into The Anderson School. A mirror image of the business world itself, Anderson faculty members took little notice of any changes and remained largely unconcerned. Many of the RCM principles—the decentralization of cost and revenue control—had been in use for a least a decade. But faculty members in the other simulation units, the Division of Physical Sciences at the College of Letters and Science and the Graduate School of Education and Information Studies, reacted with suspicion and hostility to the business principles they were being asked to embrace. To many, the new language of customers, products, outputs, and markets applied to an academic milieu was offensive. An education professor complained: "Talking about students as customers is obnoxious. I mean they aren't customers. They're students. That kind of language just doesn't belong in an educational institution."

Most faculty members had been buffered from financial dealings by a division of labor. University executives and administrators had always conducted business transactions—fundraising, marketing, and financial planning. But in the mid-1990s' environment this arrangement, well-intentioned as it was, revealed a distinct downside: Many faculty members had been too well sheltered and were unaware of the financial crisis facing the campus. Focus groups conducted among faculty members two years earlier had foreshadowed an astonishing lack of awareness. "We're number one," a professor proclaimed. "If nothing's broken, there's no need to fix it." "There's no crisis here," exclaimed another. Two years later, when budget cuts began to penetrate the academic core, many faculty members believed the crisis had been manufactured by administration to gain control. An academic senate leader confided, "This is just the beginning. RCM will strip the faculty of any power we have." A physics professor worried, "This shift to a corporate culture will allow the administration to tax us to get us to do things they want us to do."

Ideologically, many faculty members were contemptuous of business and held corporate values in low regard. One professor described a recent conversation with a vice chancellor. "Every time I talk to him, he talks about money and a marketing plan. This is not a business. I'm simply not enthusiastic about participating in boardroom culture." Another professor said:

> I don't want us to become a nation of shopkeepers. As soon as we do, we'll start thinking about things in different ways – 'my money, your costs.' We'll have to use a different vocabulary and I'm not sure we can handle the change.

Other faculty members were concerned that harsh business practices would surely follow RCM, irrevocably altering university life. A survey of one unit revealed that more than a quarter of the faculty felt that RCM would lead to staff layoffs. One professor, describing his fears, said, "In the future we may become just like business—greater reliance on part-time workers and job sharing. I see a much less comfortable world than the one we've been used to."

The boundary that had historically protected the academic community from the outside world had now become blurred. There was a great apprehension that RCM and its supporters would run roughshod over cherished academic values and reduce the university to a business. "This number crunching," exclaimed one worried professor, "will begin to drive decision-making. This administration thinks we're a business that just happens to be education."

Faculty skepticism and resistance to RCM became palpable. As the resistance intensified, the chancellor announced plans to retire, and any remaining momentum faltered. The new chancellor, who took over in 1997, apparently wished to avoid alienating the faculty, especially over something as sensitive and complex as RCM, which he had no hand in shaping. While RCM appears to have had a positive impact on some of the university's outdated fiscal procedures, it ultimately failed to penetrate the academic core.

Strategic planning with the academic senate. In 1996, seeing that RCM was failing, the administration began laying groundwork for strategic planning that would be done jointly with the academic senate. It was envisioned as a system that would reward schools and departments for demonstrating their responsiveness to changing external needs while managing their revenues and expenses. Administrators hoped that it would also provide incentives for deans to bring chairs, faculty members, and other stakeholders into the planning process at the department level (and provide penalties for deans who did not). Budget hearings would become more open, enabling the chancellor to discuss allocation decisions with a broad range of academic and administrative leaders, avoiding the secrecy that had historically surrounded the process. But, as our studies of the academic units show, this strategic planning, like RCM, failed to interest or engage the faculty.

Admissions

As noted above, faculty members have been effectively sheltered from the budgetary side of academic life, though pressures to decentralize planning and budgeting have begun to be felt at the academic unit level. Another area that serves to buffer faculty members from changes in the larger environment is undergraduate admissions, which selects nearly 4,000 new students each year, most of whom enter as freshmen.

Despite its mundane image, the admissions process is anything but. The passage of Proposition 209 in 1997 and subsequent policies promulgated by the UC board of regents to halt affirmative action has made it increasingly difficult for UCLA to maintain a diverse student body. Not surprisingly, intense politics infuses the process and the office of undergraduate admissions and relations with schools frequently is drawn into the fray. Since 1997, UCLA has invested significant resources to recruit and select a balanced pool of applicants, and the undergraduate admissions office has done most of the work.

Recruiting and enrolling the desired number of qualified students in the right categories depends on setting and meeting accurate enrollment targets. A campus committee that works with UC system-wide enrollment planning sets such targets. UCLA does not admit students on the basis of their prospective major fields of study. However, student choices do ultimately affect the internal distribution of academic resources.

In addition to its work with system-wide planners, the admissions office serves a gatekeeping function with two types of feeder schools to maintain quality. First, it works with the 1,200 or so high schools in California. Second, it maintains connections with the community colleges. The California Master Plan for Higher Education allocates graduating high school seniors to the University of California system, the California State University system, and the community college system. The master plan also provides for student transfers from community colleges and the state university campuses to University of California campuses, which requires a mechanism for coordinating curricula and credits. At UCLA, the admissions office oversees that mechanism. The admissions director also spends substantial time educating the news media and external UCLA constituencies about UCLA's recruitment and enrollment goals and the complexity of the admissions process.

Business Enterprises

As the result of reduced state support, increased competition for other resources, and increased costs of operation, UCLA has gradually moved toward operating many of its activities as financially self-supporting enterprises much like a private corporation. According to top administrators, the effect has been to reduce costs and produce a positive revenue stream from which the entire university benefits. Another impact has been the introduction of a business mind-set to at least some of the university's operations.

In 1997, all of UCLA's business functions—including student dormitories, campus food services, mail services, insurance and worker's compensation, purchasing, and financing—were consolidated under an assistant vice chancellor. Today, these activities are run as if they were part of a private corporation. The official who heads the operation (called business and financial services) joked, "We do everything the private sector does except provide a dividend." To meet student expectations, student dormitories have had to be upgraded with air conditioning and access to the Internet ($6 million was spent to retrofit student rooms with data lines). Food services at the dorms also were drastically overhauled (a $6 million cost to rehabilitate one dormitory alone) to keep pace with student and parent demands. The trend reflects a growing attitude of students who expect to be treated like customers rather than as passive entities who must take or leave whatever accommodations are offered. The official explained:

> The highest compliment I can pay someone, at least in terms of providing service, is that I call

you my customer because in my organization we
value those customers. I've got about a half a billion dollars of debt to service—no state funds, no
sterile money, it all comes from the third parties
we charge. If I don't keep all these facilities full,
I'm not operating in an appropriate fashion, I'm
not going to make my debt payments. And if I
don't make my debt payments, they don't need
me, they will get somebody else.

The office also is responsible for real estate transactions for
the campus, including off-campus development. It has responsibility for administration of extramural grants and for payroll
services. Managing real estate and off-campus development
illustrates the boundary-spanning nature of this office's functions. This official explained the process:

Well, right off the bat, I have to convince the
administration that it makes sense, so I'm across
campus with the chancellor and others. Then, I
have to go up to our [UC system-wide] treasur-
er's office and make sure I've demonstrated to
them the feasibility so we can go out and get
financing and all that. I also have to convince the
president's office to support me and I've got to
write the regents to get the thing approved and
answer any questions. I have to go to the community meetings that will require doing an environmental investigation. I have to meet with the
homeowner groups. That's my job and I have to
deal with them to allay any concerns they have
about traffic, density, and all that...

This official, who oversaw the initiative to decentralize fiscal decision-making, bringing it to the academic unit level
under Responsibility Center Management, described how the
business and financial services office continues to reshape decision-making processes at UCLA. In 1997, his office was devel-

oping a comprehensive electronic purchasing system to alleviate the roadblock created by the university's central purchasing office, which handled all transactions. He said:

> If someone wants to go out and buy a million-dollar spectrometer... that probably needs assistance of a central office. But if you were buying pens, you order them electronically. They're received the next day, and that bill is queued up in the system to make sure of our cash flows, and that we're taking advantage of our interest and leverage.

Development

With state support declining as a proportion of UCLA's total budget, and as competing institutions have become more adept at fundraising, development functions at UCLA have expanded. Development used to be analogous with an annual campaign. Now it includes a continuous year-round effort on a wide variety of fronts. Fundraisers work to acquire financial resources for a host of specialized purposes such as scholarships, endowed faculty positions, student programs, and new facilities. UCLA has been successful in building its endowment in part because it has more than 270,000 living alumni who can be called upon for financial support. The nonprofit UCLA Foundation is responsible for managing most of the funds raised.

In addition to wooing alumni, development officers spend considerable time tracking foundation giving programs in an effort to match them to UCLA's institutional needs. As part of our investigation, we interviewed officials with a variety of private foundations including MacArthur, Spencer, W. T. Grant, Andrew Mellon, Ahmanson, Keck, and The Pew Charitable Trusts. The number of foundations is on the rise, and due to the health of the equities market in past years, where much of their capital is invested, the size of their endowments and annual giving also has increased. Even among the few foundations we contacted, there was considerable variation in size of endowment and annual giving and support of basic or applied research. Much of the variation seems to stem from the peculiarities of their founders and the composition of their boards. Foundations develop relationships with universities over time and maintain relationships where they feel their investments have paid off.

When we began thinking about UCLA's environment, we assumed foundations would be considered stakeholders of the university. But we discovered that while UCLA is held in generally high regard, foundations do not depend on UCLA in the way we initially thought. Most foundation officials noted that UCLA has a strong reputation for managing its grants program professionally but that it does not necessarily have a highly visible or interdependent status with foundations that could warrant calling them stakeholders.

With regard to the university's development function, the investigation left little doubt about its growing importance as a repository of intelligence to help faculty members penetrate and understand the varied and somewhat opaque internal operations of foundations.

UCLA's development infrastructure is elaborate, with formalized processes to coordinate activities across academic units, to avert conflict between units, and to enhance the efficiency of efforts. Although it began as a single, central office, UCLA's development function more recently has been dispersed throughout campus down to the program level, placing it closer to the academic core. Now all major academic units on campus have their own development offices.

At the same time, the development office is becoming more professionalized. In earlier years, development positions often were filled with former athletes and affable, loyal alumni who had an emotional connection to the university. Today, development officers are trained specialists focused on their careers more than on the institution. One development officer explained:

> What's happened with the professionalization of
> the field is that far more often the people on the

> development side are not alumni of that school and do not commit to that particular institution for an indefinite period of 10 or 20 years... You have much more career ladder consciousness and often sort of low-middle- and upper-middle-management development officers will zigzag to get a better opportunity at other institutions. They're not itinerants, but they will make a move every five years or so.

Faculty members increasingly are called upon to participate actively in both prospecting for and working with potential donors. Not surprisingly, some professors resist engaging in development work because they do not feel it is their responsibility. An administrator in UCLA's development office acknowledged, "Some faculty members perceive us as saving their lives, while others see us with pure skepticism." UCLA's development officers frequently perform an orientation and training function for faculty members, especially department chairs. "It's about developing relationships," the administrator said. Moreover, he added, "Once faculty members see direct financial benefits for their research, they are more likely to participate willingly."

Public Information

Another unit that both connects faculty members to the environment and protects them from it is UCLA's office of media relations, which performs the university's public information function. The central media relations office is responsible for disseminating information about the university administration and campus-wide issues. In addition, as with the development function, each of the larger academic units, typically at the school or college level, has its own public information office. The trend has been to decentralize public information to the unit level. While some public information officers report directly to the central office, others are hired by and report to a dean, with a dotted-line relationship to the central office.

UCLA sets general policies or guidelines for the public information function, whose goal is not simply to inform but to create advocates, or key constituents, for the university. Public information officers perform three key functions:

1) Respond to news media inquiries about events or persons at UCLA
2) Generate publicity material, like press releases or special mailings, to promote the work being done at UCLA
3) Connect individuals or groups external to UCLA with faculty who possess certain specific kinds of expertise to which they seek access

While public information officers must field incoming media calls, the focus is on generating UCLA's own material that can be communicated directly without "media gatekeepers between us and our principal audience," as one public information officer put it. The idea is to tailor material and communication to audiences deemed important to UCLA. Public information officers retain what is called the A-list of media most important to UCLA. The A-list comprises about 40 media organizations, including the *New York Times*, *Los Angeles Times*, and the Associated Press, chosen because of their stature and the size of their readership. It also includes selected smaller local media, such as the now defunct *Santa Monica Outlook* because of its proximity to UCLA and *La Opinion*, the largest Spanish language newspaper in the Los Angeles area. Generally when a big research story comes up, the officers will place personal phone calls to selected media on the A-list alerting them to it. An official described it as "calling people in advance, letting them know it's coming, putting it right in their hands only if they really want it." Such a personalized approach tends to bind the media more closely to UCLA and make them more receptive to printing stories about the university. Not surprisingly, working effectively with the A-list requires developing personal relationships with key reporters. A communications administrator said:

If a UCLA faculty member discovers another pyramid in Egypt, we're not going to have any trouble having that story appear anywhere. But it does help for us to already know the key people in all the major media, which we do, and have ongoing relationships with them. It's not going to make that story any easier. But when a story requires explanation… so a reporter understands why it's important, or even if it's a great story but it's coming in with the flood of all the other great stories, that's when it (a personal relationship) really does become quite valuable.

In the past few years, UCLA has placed a high priority on public information officers working directly with faculty members to expose their work to the larger world. These internal relationships also help public information officers direct inquiries from the media to faculty members who can help them. For instance, within the College of Letters and Science, the two information officers deal routinely with about 200 of about 1,000 faculty members, issuing press releases about their work or directing media calls to them. A faculty communication project calls on the deans to help identify the faculty who are doing work with public appeal. An information officer said:

We want to make sure that we keep connected to them, explore all of their research, know what they're doing… and then we can exploit it as best we can, and make sure that what they're doing is part of our communications process.

From the information officers' perspective, it is a matter of building trust with the faculty as well as with the media. Thus, trusting personal relationships are vital to their success. Information officers in the central media relations office tend to rely on their academic unit counterparts—who are physically and professionally closer to professors—for detailed knowledge of and access to faculty members.

The public information function is part of UCLA's umbrella external affairs organization—known at the time of our investigation as university relations. As one UCLA official noted, public information is only part of a larger picture:

> Now we've become an information conduit to the world, and we're glad to do that. That's an important part of what we do. But it's not the driving force, and it's not the mission statement of university relations. University relations exists to create advocates, and part of that is good relationships with the media. But that is not the goal.

How Environmental Changes Affect UCLA

This investigation of UCLA's environment reveals how its environment is becoming increasingly complex and competitive. To retain stability, the University of California system must control individual campuses in their exchanges with the political environment so that the university appears to speak with a single voice. But, at the same time, because of the rapidity of change, it now encourages individual campuses and faculty members to forge their own relationships with political actors to ensure a continuing share of resources. As more actors become engaged with UCLA, its boundaries become increasingly permeable. As exchanges increase, administrators try to buffer campuses and the technical core (faculty members) from the intrusion of outside forces.

Most of the important environmental changes are being driven by reductions in public funding and resulting changes in stakeholders' expectations of UCLA. At the same time, funding from private foundations has grown, but competition for private funds has increased because of growing demand. Because of these conditions, the decline in state support has produced an increase in the transaction costs of acquiring each dollar of support.

Student fees have been raised substantially in the past decade, so political reality makes it unlikely that they will be increased further, at least in the near term. An effect of higher student fees has been to encourage students, parents, and elected officials to demand more value from dollars spent. In turn, stakeholders are holding the university more accountable, questioning faculty teaching loads and expecting higher levels of overall performance putting increased demands on administrators who find themselves positioned between these forces and the faculty.

Many faculty members seem unaware of changes in the environment. This may be the result of steps that UCLA has taken to adapt—bolstering the infrastructure around research, and expanding development, media relations-public information, and government relations—and which have also served to insulate the faculty. While it is too early to determine the impact of these changes, they may auger a power shift away from the faculty toward these buffering functions.

We now turn to an examination of the three academic units to observe how environmental pressures, some buffered by the university, affect and shape its core academic operations.

References

Whalen, E. (1991). *Responsibility center management.* Bloomington, IN: Indiana University Press.

3

The Anderson School

The Anderson School is located in a striking, modern-style building known as the Anderson Complex on the north end of the UCLA campus. Built in 1995, the terra cotta, Romanesque structure consists of seven buildings connected with pathways and bridges. Described in Anderson's brochures as "the most technologically sophisticated business school in the nation," the school is home to about 80 tenure-track faculty members, 54 visiting or adjunct professors, and a 230-member support staff.

The school offers three MBA programs. The largest, enrolling more than 600 students each year, is the regular full-time MBA program, designed for students with limited managerial experience to prepare them for the business world. Two part-time programs are geared for professionals. The Fully-Employed MBA (FEMBA) enrolls about 400 professionals who work full-time and take courses in the afternoons and on weekends. The Executive MBA (EMBA) has about 140 executives who already have substantial experience in their fields. The school also offers a small doctoral program of about 70 students. While Anderson does not offer an undergraduate business degree, it does provide an undergraduate accounting minor that enrolls about 300 students. Recently, the school has been expanding its Executive Education Program—an important source of new revenue—that provides continuing education to approximately 1,300 executives each year, but no terminal degree.

The school is organized as a single management department with nine academic disciplines, or areas. They include:
- Accounting
- Business economics
- Decision sciences
- Finance

- Human resources and organizational behavior
- Information systems
- Marketing
- Operations and technology management
- Strategy and organization

They range in size from five to 20 faculty members.

Academic Life

Anderson School faculty members come from a diverse set of backgrounds. One professor explained:

> Unlike any other school or department I know, the faculty doesn't share a common discipline or common training. If you go to law school, pretty much everyone has a law degree. If you go to an economics department, pretty much everyone has an economics degree. But among our faculty, somewhere between 15 and 20 different degrees are represented.

Most faculty members say they did not set out to become business school professors but rather found their way to the university on unexpected paths. Some began as engineers, while others started out as psychologists, economists, or chemists. Enrolling in an MBA program to enhance their careers, they found they had natural talents and an affinity for academic work. Others started out as management consultants and became deeply interested in management and business problems. Still others were attracted to scientific inquiry. Pursuing a PhD was a natural next step. One recalled:

> I was attracted to the science part of it. I don't care whether managers learn to run their companies better or not, but I do like the study of organizations. It doesn't help me relate to MBAs, but it helps keep me happy anyway.

Most professors say they find academic life enormously satisfying. Much of their satisfaction comes from freedom to control their research agenda and their time. When asked "Who determines what you choose to study?" one faculty member exclaimed, "Me! Two hundred percent!" Another professor explained further, "You work hard, but you set your own hours. To a large extent you determine your own teaching. And, there is minimal paperwork—you determine the agenda."

When professors compare their academic lives to the corporate world, most agree they are happy where they are because they would not fit the corporate mold. One said, "I don't make a very good employee in the traditional sense because I don't like other people to organize my energies." Another elaborated on the regimentation of the corporate world:

> I had enough summer jobs and I was in the military for awhile, and that's pretty regimented. And I could see that the corporate world was not going to be as bad as the military, but pretty close.

While these business professors set their own hours, most complain about the limits of time. One professor said:

> The biggest obstacle to getting my research done is probably time. But you know, I do it to myself … so I'm the biggest culprit, okay? There's just simply not enough time to do everything that you want to do. So you have to pick really interesting topics.

Despite their autonomy, professors work long hours, working an average of nine hours each day not counting Fridays, Saturdays, or Sundays. Slightly more than a third (37%) is spent on research, another third (32%) is devoted to teaching, and about 20% to service. The rest of the time is split between mentoring, professional development, and other activities. About two-thirds (65%) of their working time is spent on campus—the rest is used at home or in the field.

Even with heavy workloads, most professors keep regular hours on campus. One said: "I come in and work five days a week, 8:30 to 5:00, and Saturday until 3:00. And that's it." Another described his surprisingly long hours:

> I come in here, get here at about 8:00, stay 'til 6. I do that seven days a week. On Saturdays and Sundays, I usually get in an hour later and leave a little early.

Others work a later shift, arriving at 10 a.m. but staying until 7 or 8 p.m. One professor described this routine:

> I come here around 10, 10:30, try to be here 'til about 9, 9:30 in the evening. Get my work done, go home. I have a pretty late dinner and then work for about an hour or two, depending on the particular day… seven days a week.

Anderson School professors know that they work longer than most of their colleagues in other departments. One acknowledged:

> I tend to have an 8:00 to 6:00 schedule in the office everyday. So do most of the people in my area. That's atypical for the university. But that's just the culture we have here.

Despite the large investment of time in being on campus and the demands of their research, most professors say they derive intense satisfaction from their teaching. One said:

> The biggest kick comes from the fact that if you've been able to convince a few people in the class who were able to see things because you've said something or you discussed things with them and they could say, 'Ah hah. I see it now.' That's very satisfying—to know at the end of the quarter, there are a few people, at least, who saw it in a way they hadn't thought about before.

But, according to many faculty members, though they like teaching it can also be taxing, especially as MBA students become more demanding. One professor explained:

> If you teach a core course, you can write off that whole quarter. You have to spend the entire time writing the lectures and holding their hands. The students are unusually demanding.

To offset strains like this, most faculty members enjoy interacting with their colleagues. Faculty members in finance eat lunch with each other every day. One finance professor said:

> My group goes for lunch together every day. It's both eating lunch and discussing research, sometimes issues related to the department and the school. So it's a good time to meet each other and find out what's going on around us.

A fact that is not lost on most UCLA faculty members not part of the Anderson School is that Anderson professors are paid substantially more than professors in most other fields (medicine excepted). "It's what the market can bear. What we could earn in private industry is the benchmark," said one professor.

Not surprisingly, these professors are mostly content with their compensation, even though most know they could earn more in private industry. One professor explained:

> When you ask me, 'Do I think I'm fairly compensated?' I say yes. And do I think $190,000 a year for a senior faculty is a lot of money? Yes. But the fact of the matter is other people are offering $300,000 and we don't.

Others compare their salaries with colleagues at Harvard, Stanford, Chicago, and other private schools, which makes them unhappy. One faculty member said:

> Senior faculty members here get paid much less than they do at top private schools. You combine

that with the fact that Los Angeles is a very
expensive place to live, that California has the
highest state taxes in the country right next to
New York, and basically the standard of living for
a senior finance faculty member in California is
very poor.

But overall, the trade-off of greater autonomy for less salary
is a trade that most seem happy to make. One professor
explained:

I feel that I'm compensated equitably within the
system. I have no complaints about that. On several occasions I've gotten offers from the industry
which I turned down, and my father never did
understand that. He said, 'How could you forgo
that amount of income?' But you know, that's the
trade-off we make.

The Work of Research and Teaching

To manage a university, whether as a high-level administrator,
or as an academic leader like a department chair requires a clear
understanding of how the work of the university (research and
teaching) actually gets done. These processes transform inputs
(students, resources, political support) into outputs (graduates,
research products, and community service). More important,
these processes structure each academic unit's day-to-day work
that give shape and support to its culture. As we discovered in
our industrial studies, companies like Hewlett Packard and
New United Motor Manufacturing, Inc. (NUMMI) that successfully exchanged mass production for flexible work systems
where employees participated in decisions also established the
beginning of new and productive human cultures required to
support them.

From our work within UCLA we began to see how these
same ideas apply to higher education: To alter academic culture
requires leaders to make improvements in the work systems

that, in turn, require different behavior, assumptions, and beliefs to function. The trouble was, as we shall see, we found these processes to be largely opaque. To make them visible was the first step. It required us to ferret them out with help from key informants within each of the academic units. We mapped them out, step-by-step, and then subjected the results to a validity check—is this how it really looks?—in each unit.

Before we turn to a discussion of these processes, we describe a typical day in the life of a faculty member to give the reader a sense of how they regard their careers. Despite faculty members' attempts to keep research days separate from teaching days, they tend to run together. However, for the ease of discussion we have divided the following discussion into somewhat artificial research and teaching days. In the Anderson School it is a common practice to double-up, teaching two classes for two quarters in a row (the normal load is four courses each year), freeing up the third quarter plus the summer to create a six-month block of time devoted to research.

Research

A Typical Research Day

Most faculty members are clear in their preference for research days as opposed to those days they are teaching. One professor explained:

> I've been on sabbatical for a year, so mostly I've had these research days. It has been a delight. On those days, what is permitted that's not permitted on the mixed days is kind of an overindulgence in research without the discipline of having to prepare for class and attend office hours. I can spend as much time as I want on my research.

Faculty members conduct their research in a variety of ways. Some prefer working at home because of the peace and isolation it affords. Others prefer to work at the university because of the resources available and because the environment is more conducive to working. Having books and the library nearby and computers that are often faster and more powerful than those they have at home make working on campus more attractive. For others, coming into the office provides a sense of discipline that is hard to find at home. One explained why he values working on campus:

> Mostly I think it's just for discipline. I'm here 8:00 to 6:00, just like a bureaucrat. I come in here and I work. I don't come here and turn on the CD player or read novels. I work here. That's what gets done here.

When they arrive at the office, most professors first check their email and voice messages. Then they begin working on their research that may include a number of separate projects, each with its own schedule and priority. One professor described how he works:

> After checking email, I'll check the computer if I've been running a program overnight. Then I'd just work on whatever research project I'm working on. At any given time I'm working on multiple projects with multiple people, but I try to prioritize them. For example, I just had a review for a second revision back from a paper, so I want to get that one published. So that goes to the top of the queue because it came back. So today, I'm working on responses to reviewers and writing analyses. And I'm talking to one of my coauthors at Stanford.

Many faculty members comment that research is always on their minds, making it difficult to leave work at the office. One noted, "It's just the nature of the job. If you've been working on a model during the day and at night you think, what if I changed that part of the model... it just comes into your head." For this reason, many faculty members find it hard to leave work behind on the weekends. One explained:

What I like to do on weekends is flow in and out
of work. My work is set up in my home office. I
may float into it for an hour or two, float out of it
and do something with the family, or work out,
or go watch a basketball game, some such thing,
float back in. It doesn't feel like work then.
Sometimes, quite frankly, I'd much rather be
spending time on academic matters than watch
some silly TV show.

The Research Process

In the Anderson School, and in the other academic units we
studied, the research process was hard to discern. It seemed
to operate almost unconsciously as though directed by a hidden hand. Ferreting out precisely how these processes work
was difficult because most faculty members do not think of
their research as a process. Nevertheless, while the way in
which Anderson School faculty members conduct their
research is highly varied, it can be seen as having six essential
steps.

Generate ideas. First, a problem or idea must be generated.
Problems arise from a variety of sources—from conversations
with colleagues or students, from books or articles. One professor said he got his best ideas from his dreams. Another faculty
member described how his research ideas arise:

My ideas might come while I'm thinking about
problems we don't understand, or for which we
don't have good answers. They might come up
in a teaching context, trying to explain something to students and realizing that I don't
understand it myself. They could be from a sem-
inar when somebody brings something up that I
don't think I am understanding, and I go and
read the literature, and I don't find it explicit
enough. So ideas come from reading, thinking,
and talking to people.

As discussed earlier, professors are virtually autonomous in deciding what to study. Tenured professors can even pursue domains outside the field of business. One explained, "They'll never stop you from researching something just because it doesn't fit within the business school." Another said, "I have enormous, complete autonomy. If I want to study the sounds that whales make, I can do it."

Non-tenured professors' freedom is somewhat tempered because they know they ultimately will be judged on the path they chose to follow. One assistant professor said, "Autonomy is relative. After six years, when the tenure step comes, they [the senior faculty] decide whether they liked the things you did or not."

Find resources. Once a faculty member has a good idea he or she needs to find resources to do the work. Compared to other academic units, Anderson professors spend little time worrying about resources and writing grant proposals. The reason is that revenue retained from student fees is redistributed to the academic staff for research. According to one professor this pattern is similar across business schools:

> Generally speaking, business schools are not funded by grants. If you go to the top business schools, you'll find that research is funded by the school itself. Most faculty in, say, psychology basically get a nine-month salary and they supplement that with grants from NSF [National Science Foundation] and so on. In contrast, we basically get a 12-month salary: a nine-month salary plus a three-month summer supplement.

The dean elaborated on some of the reasons that research is supported in this fashion:

> We now have the capability to raise so much money from fees that the competition is more of a marketplace competition [rather than competing with the rest of the UCLA campus for the state's allocation]. A relatively small amount [of

our total budget] comes from the state, but [tuition] is what funds our faculty salaries.

Some professors, especially those who do theoretical work, explain that they do not require much outside support. One faculty member elaborated, saying, "I do research that doesn't take big databases. Or I do theory pieces. Or I do epistemology. You don't have to collect data for that." Another faculty added, "If you're a theoretician, a very good one, you can produce a paper from scratch in your office, never leave your office. You don't even need a computer. You just write and it's all done."

Even professors who conduct empirical work say they need little in the way of funding. One marketing professor explained:

> I think I could probably speak for almost everyone. Most fields in the business school, most of their research is not dollar intensive. It's just not. There are people who do more behavioral research that involves running experiments, but typically they're done with undergraduates. You give them $10 and they fill something out. So it's small pockets of money, and we can usually fund that from within our department.

Some of the professors say that foundations and government agencies think there may be a conflict of interest in supporting research on business. One said:

> There are no agencies that give a lot of money for business studies. There are some, but the amount of funding available is small. There is also suspicion from the rest of campus. They say, 'These guys [in the business school] are working on business. We have to go out and get money. They're talking about making money. So how can that be research?' It's a concern about the separation between church and state. They think we're too close to the money.

Locate a database. Once an idea has crystallized and financial support is in hand, most professors go through what they describe as a preparatory phase. Mostly this means locating and readying a database for analysis. Most say they rely on secondary data for their research, analyzing data that have already been collected. Often such data exist as part of a company's financial records or as marketing data gathered from the bar codes on supermarket products. Professors also use databases purchased by the school or downloaded free from the web. In other cases, professors work from data they collected as part of consulting projects. One marketing professor explained:

> All of the data that I use is secondary data, preexisting data available to people for purchase. So I don't do any primary data collection. Once in a while I might do a survey, a small survey or something. But almost all of the research I do now is either analytical or it doesn't use data, or if it does use data, it uses data that I've previously collected.

Test real-world problems. Once data are secured, Anderson professors use computers to search for patterns or model and test real-world problems. Often, analyses that create models and simulations require software programs such as Mathematica or Statistical Package for the Social Sciences (SPSS). One professor of business economics explained:

> I do a lot of computer work, sort of numerical simulations. So a lot of my time is spent coding. Basically I set up somewhat artificial economies where I have lots of different actors in these economies, and I try to see how they would interact. Most of my work has to do with trying to understand how markets aggregate individual behavior. And since a lot of the work is technically demanding, the only way you can look at these issues is through computer-type simulations.

Professors often conduct experiments and analyses using computer-generated models. One professor who studies supply-chain management explained:

> One of the things I've been reading is that customers in supply chains don't have good information about the others' cost structure. So how can they coordinate properly without knowing what the other guy is up to? You can do some simple experiments using spreadsheets to model both parties' behavior. But you don't actually know what type the other guy is. So you can say if he is type A, or type B, or type C—you can make a whole bunch of graphs of what all the different types could be. You can determine what the total profits or the inventory levels or whatever in the supply side should be, depending on how the other person is behaving. That's just a very rough description.

Write up the results. Once the data are analyzed, professors spend anywhere from six months to several years writing up the results (papers tend to run between 20 and 30 pages). If it is a collaborative effort with colleagues or students, authors divide up the writing responsibilities, meet periodically, and exchange drafts via email. Often, drafts are presented at conferences where they are subjected to criticism and revised. One professor cautioned against this strategy because, "If you give a lot of presentations on the same paper and it never turns into an article, it counts against you."

Publish the results. Finally, most papers eventually find their way into a publication. And, as in other departments, published works in recognized, peer-reviewed journals are required for advancement. Each business specialty has two or three top tier journals that are refereed and publish only a fraction of the manuscripts that they receive. These are the journals to which professors aspire because, as one explained, "Nothing else counts. Published papers are number one, and papers published in top journals carry more weight."

But getting a paper published can be long and arduous. Once a paper is submitted, professors may wait from several months to a year for a response. And in most fields, submitting the same paper to multiple journals at the same time is considered taboo. One professor explained:

> If you submit a paper in January, the next October you may be writing, 'Dear so and so, it's been ten months since I submitted my paper entitled so and so. Is there any word of progress?' Three more months pass and (the editor) says, 'We're working on it.'

Papers are rarely accepted on the first try. Often, publishers ask professors to "revise and resubmit" their papers to incorporate criticisms made in the reviewing process. Or, a journal may reject a paper outright causing professors to quickly submit it to another journal for consideration. Professors complain about the subjective nature of publishers' decisions to publish or reject. Many told us stories about papers that were rejected by one journal, only to be accepted by—and sometimes win awards from—another.

Teaching

A Typical Teaching Day

During the quarters in which faculty members organize their teaching, it dominates their lives. One professor notes, "On days I teach, I get virtually no research done." A few are able to squeeze in an hour or two of research in the morning so they don't lose touch with their projects. Most, however, consciously put research on hold so they can devote themselves to teaching. One explained:

> During teaching quarters, I teach three classes— two MBA classes and a PhD-level class. And basically preparing and teaching takes up the whole quarter, so research is put on the back burner.

Another faculty member discussed other reasons for keeping the two separate:

> You work in a different way when you're teaching. Your whole orientation is different. When you're teaching, you're constantly putting out. When you're doing research, you need peace and quiet.

Teaching days are shaped around the time professors actually spend in the classroom. Even if faculty members have taught a class many times, they typically spend at least an hour preparing either just before class, or the night before. Professors often get to class several minutes early to organize their material, queue up videos, and make sure that the fancy electronics are ready to go.

After class, professors often spend time recording students' grades for participation, grading exams or papers, or holding office hours. From beginning to end, for most professors, teaching days are dedicated to the students. One professor said, "On teaching days I'm on public view, and I face structured tasks that I have to finish." Another said, "On days I'm teaching, I usually teach four hours a day. Then I usually have office hours that day. So really the whole day is involvement with students."

The Teaching Process

Compared to research, the teaching process is quite straightforward. One of the reasons for its relative simplicity is that MBA classes are arranged like a cafeteria and easy to standardize. Also, because evaluations are important, as they translate into rankings and income, the Anderson School puts a high priority on well-organized teaching. The process of preparing and teaching courses that have been on the books for a while is shorter than for new courses. And, preparing core courses usually takes longer than electives because of the need to meet and confer among faculty members.

As a first step in the process, a new course must be initiated by a group of faculty members who also have to justify the reasons for it. But courses like Principles of Marketing that are old standbys and have been listed in the curriculum for years undergo periodic reevaluation. Others, especially electives and seminars, may remain listed in the catalog even if they have not been taught for years, but revived when new faculty members express interest in them.

Anderson School professors are estimated to change about 10% to 15% of the content of their courses from year to year, which roughly equates to a complete overhaul of the curriculum every ten years. According to one professor, this is an appropriate renewal rate. "A total cycle time of seven to ten years for a business school is about right," he said. "We're not the English department. We can't teach the same thing for hundreds of years."

Student demand for courses is determined partly through a process known as bidding—that, because of its business-like philosophy, would probably offend faculty members in other departments. At the beginning of each quarter, students receive false currency called Anderson dollars they use to buy courses. Professors present their upcoming courses to students in a large meeting when they bid for classes they want. In this way, professors can determine the market value of their courses before they are offered. One explained:

> This is a free market for courses. If the students don't like your courses they won't come. It's very simple and very honest. After all, they're the people who are paying… So you find out very directly who wants what. And there are lots of people offering lots of good courses. It's a very competitive market… You can even find out the marginal price of the last bid on your course. So you know what your course is valued at in the internal marketplace. Second-year students who have less time left get more dollars.

Teaching a core MBA course, according to most faculty members, is demanding and takes a good deal of advance preparation. Core courses usually seat 60 or 70 students compared to 23 on average in the elective courses. And several sections taught by different professors are usually running at once. Professors meet before the beginning of each course to calibrate syllabi, schedules, textbooks, and cases so that sections are interchangeable. Once the quarter is underway, professors often continue meeting on a weekly basis to discuss progress and exams.

Like many business schools, the Anderson School incorporates the case method into most of its courses, although this varies somewhat by area. For instance, cases are used more heavily in strategy and less in marketing and operations. Many cases come from the Harvard Business School Press. While some faculty members favor using newer cases, others are comfortable using older ones because fundamental business problems tend to remain the same over time. One faculty member explained:

> There's a lot of inertia in systems and institutions. So part of it is paying attention to the fundamentals and saying, 'Well, even though this case is 1986, the same problem exists today. And you know, here it is in Company X or Company Y.' So older cases can be easily updated just by referencing current problems in current companies. Students are typically fine with that, as long as the whole course isn't largely dated material. And then we also position the really old stuff as 'classics.'

Most courses are taught in the new complex's modern amphitheaters that seat 70 students. Typical classes appear as carefully choreographed performances. A popular format is to mix cases and lectures, using PowerPoint slides to illustrate and give life to the material. Some professors prepare prints of their overheads for students before class, while some distribute them later so students see them for the first time during class. The purpose, according to one professor, is to produce a "higher level of drama!"

All students display name cards on their desks so professors get to know their names, although some professors say they try to learn students' names by heart early in the quarter. One professor explained why:

> I try to memorize their names because they forget their cards. Or even if they bring name cards, they're often obscured by someone in front. So if you don't know their names, you end up saying, "You!" Or you sort of crane your neck around to see the card. It gives a strong signal that the instructor doesn't know anybody.

Professors teaching in the Fully-Employed MBA program take care to know their professional students because, in some cases, the students—or the companies for which they work—are the subject of the cases under discussion.

Teaching responsibilities extend beyond the classrooms into providing students with quick feedback on their performance. Professors explain that they attempt to grade and return papers within two weeks—an expectation reinforced by anxious students. One professor explained:

> It is very important that you get your feedback to them. Whenever I get papers back to them within a week, they seem to really appreciate it. Two weeks is tolerated. If it goes longer than two weeks, they may not say, 'Where's our stuff?' but they're disappointed. They want their feedback. Needless to say, getting 55 papers back in a week is not an easy task.

Professors also hold office hours several times each week, although these face-to-face meetings are slowly being replaced by email exchanges. One faculty member explained:

> I'd say the predominant mode of contact outside of class between students and faculty is now email. So email usually determines whether a meeting is necessary. Students are pretty good

about using the break during class or at the end of class time to get their questions in. So typically you won't see students during office hours.

Feedback on the Processes

Compared to the other academic units, as we shall see later in this book, the Anderson School regularly uses feedback from students to regulate the teaching process. But feedback from research results is not so direct, largely because of its complexity. Nevertheless, many faculty members remain concerned about the impact their research has in the larger world and, as we shall see, fault the university for an overly narrow definition of what qualifies as research.

Feedback on Teaching

Students evaluate courses as part of the bidding process to determine their market value. Courses are also evaluated by faculty members while they are teaching by monitoring students' interactions and questions, and from the quality of students' written work. At the end of each quarter, courses are again assessed using student evaluation forms.

Some professors seek more student feedback and come up with creative evaluation methods. For example, one professor borrowed an idea from Total Quality Management and created a five-student quality circle. He met with them regularly over lunch at the faculty center during the quarter to solicit their feedback. Other professors design their own evaluation forms and get student feedback while the course is being taught so they can make corrections while the class is in progress.

Feedback on Research Results

The impact of professors' research is more difficult to assess because of the complex path that some new ideas travel. And, because of their varied background, faculty members engage in an equally wide variety of research—from research that has clear practical implications for companies to theoretical model-building. In any case, the standard assessment of the quality of faculty research is whether or not papers are accepted for publication in a scholarly journal. Another measure—also used as a proxy for impact—is the degree to which professors are perceived as having voice in their fields. A third measure is the number of times articles are cited in other publications. But the Anderson School dean maintains the important measure is whether or not professors' research goes beyond books and journal articles, and changes how the public thinks. He explained:

> Take a look around you. When you say things like, 'I want to keep my options open' or 'What's the bottom line?' or 'Don't put all your eggs in one basket; you need to diversify your risks.' Or even the entire notion of human capital—those all emanated from management. You even see it in presidential campaign speeches. This is our most important product, particularly if you think about output of a business school industry. There was a great op-ed piece in the L.A. Times a few weeks ago. It talked about where candidates went when they ran out of ideas—they went to management consultants! So management informs public thinking.

Other professors point out that business schools have been at the heart of improving national productivity and that they are influential in shaping the emerging information economy. One said:

> Over the past few decades the money flowed into business schools because we were putting out a valuable perspective... The U.S. is ten times more efficient today than we were 20 years ago. Now, in the history of the world, there has never been a more prosperous moment that is linked to a radical change in thinking about commerce and efficiency. Business schools are at the center of the changing nature of commerce.

In some cases, research has clear practical outcomes. One marketing professor, for example, developed a software package based on an analysis of consumer buying patterns. Grocery stores use his software to target promotional campaigns. Or, as another professor pointed out, research can help identify emerging economic and social trends, such as pressures for corporations to become more socially responsible. One senior faculty member explained how his research helps society run more efficiently:

> I've worked for 30 or 40 of the Fortune 500 companies—companies like Mobil, Chevron, Kellogg's, Mars, UNOCAL, and TRW. They have adopted my algorithms for truck driving, production scheduling, and this sort of stuff. So the benefit is that they've saved one hell of a lot of money, and your groceries are a hell of a lot cheaper.

Others hope that their research will have a direct application to business practice in the future. One professor said:

> Most of my research doesn't have any sort of obvious direct application, but because the idea is to improve the way we solve problems—not any particular problem, but sort of a whole set of problems—then indirectly it affects business practice. My work is more methodological and so I kind of expect that the fruits of this research will be harvested at some point down the road by other people.

Some professors are critical of the university's insistence that research must be published in academic journals. Because most journals are read by so few, and those readers are most likely to be other faculty members, this requirement prevents research from having a direct impact. One said:

> The measure for success is publication in recognized theoretical journals—secondarily, citations by other researchers. I now feel that that's a

closed system. It can be so closed as to have almost no impact on the rest of the world.

In fact, some professors say academe's incentive system keeps them trapped and prevents them from reaching a broader audience. One explained:

> At this point, the people affected by my research are primarily other academics like me. Eventually I'm getting into data I think that some of the consulting firms will be interested in. Like I'm looking at the speed with which certain accounting innovations wander through industry and the reasons why they do that. I mean, that's good sort of general academic stuff that no firm in its right mind would care about except a consultant. So this is primarily purely academic stuff. And that's to a certain extent because the 1-A journals publish only purely academic stuff. So I'm stuck. It has to be purely academic to get into the journals because that's all they use to evaluate your tenure status here.

Another professor explained that the traditional publishing requirement rewards narrow and unimaginative research at the expense of bold work that promises breakthroughs in thinking. He elaborated:

> [The school] is struggling as I see it with too narrow a focus of what research is and how it should be rewarded. It seems to me that the successful management professor of the future—the one who should be rewarded—provides a very rich blend of academic contributions and managerial contributions. The research gets published in good journals but is also translated into actionable items for executives or for MBA students or executive MBAs. Some of us do that. I think I do that. And I feel appreciated here. I don't have a

problem with this school, but I feel that in the future we're going to have to do more of that and look more at that blend. I see us over-reward very narrow definitions of research. So, what academic excellence is in a professional school such as ours needs to be redefined.

Some professors, however, downplay the contribution of business school research to society altogether. One noted:

We are not doing physics here. We are not making fundamental contributions to fundamental knowledge. That would be very satisfying. But we are in the happy position of being able to really contribute on a daily basis by teaching students, working with students, which is quite productive.

External Pressures for Change

Now with a snapshot of the Anderson School culture in mind, and an understanding of how its key processes (research and teaching) actually work, we move to a discussion of how the school actually responds to changes in its environment. We were particularly lucky in being at the school while it was in crisis. We say lucky because the crisis caused administrators and faculty members to let down their guard, enabling us to see not only what they said, but also what they did under stressful circumstances.

Over the past decade, the school has been buffeted by two main forces. First, competition among business schools has increased dramatically. In addition to aggressive student recruiting, top east coast schools—like Harvard and MIT—have set up west coast operations to cut into the west coast schools' market. And, not unexpectedly, some west coast schools are setting up operations in the east. Second, the proportion of state revenue that flows into the school continues to decline. Together, these forces have driven the Anderson School, perhaps faster than others, down a path of privatization. As we shall soon see, it has arrived, but not without controversy.

Competition among Business Schools

Competition has intensified among business schools as each tries to increase its prestige and become MBA students' school of choice. In the business school world, being competitive means being among the top ranked schools, a status conferred by *Business Week* and *U.S. News & World Report*.

In 1988, *Business Week* published its first nationwide business school ranking. Rankings were based on surveys of Fortune 500 employers who hire new MBAs and on graduates' evaluation of their educational experience. For the first time, business schools had been evaluated on something other than faculty scholarship. One Anderson professor remembered:

> It was a watershed event—the fall of 1988 when *Business Week* published its first survey. I thought, 'this is a revolution,' because what it did was rank business schools on something other than research, having entirely to do with students' experiences and the market reaction to the students.

U.S. News & World Report soon followed suit with a survey of its own that was based on a variety of other measures including students' GMAT scores, placement rates, and faculty salaries. The *Business Week* survey seemed to receive the most attention, however, because it included students' opinions. One professor explained:

> We've had other kinds of rankings but this one [*Business Week*] is the one that is really more widely published. It's been given more hoopla, and it has this consumerist notion of asking the students to rate it.

Declining State Funding

The second major force reshaping the Anderson School is a decreasing proportion of state funds. The absolute value of the state's contribution to Anderson's budget actually increased slightly during the 1980s and 1990s, from $9.3 million in 1986, to more than $13 million in 1996. But as a proportion of Anderson's total revenue, the state's contribution fell dramatically: In 1978, state funds represented 76% of Anderson's revenue. By 1986, this figure had dropped to two-thirds (62%), and by 1993 it was down to half (49%). By 1997, state revenue had fallen to a third of the total.

The challenge for Anderson, as a public institution, was competing with top business schools, most of which are private and endowed with considerable resources. Prestige is largely a function of faculty members' status, and business schools try to raise their prestige by obtaining so-called stars, which sometimes means stealing them away from competing institutions. Without resources, it is impossible to offer the competitive salaries needed to lure top faculty, making it virtually impossible for Anderson to compete. The dean explained:

> The state is less than a third of our total budget and falling. We are competing for tuition dollars directly with Stanford and Harvard, who are far better capitalized than we are. It's difficult to compete in that crowd.

Especially in a public university, paying faculty members top business school salaries that often run into six digit figures is hard to justify. Business school administrators point to the market rate to justify such large salaries. While most Anderson School professors say they do not want to work in the corporate world, the market rate is still used as a rationale for their large salaries. And to attract new faculty members, the school must offer close to what they could earn in the private sector. One professor explained:

> The salaries have been driven by the fact that there are things we do here in the management school that have value to the private sector, and so people do have choices, and that drives up their salaries. Faculty salaries have gone up, and competition for the best faculty has grown more intense. So, to have the best students and to have the best faculty, we need resources.

As costs increased and public revenue dwindled, the school had to find new sources of revenue. The obvious possibilities were private gifts, endowments, and alumni support. None of these, however, was considered viable for the long run because they require a concerted and expensive fundraising effort. While the school brought in millions with a fundraising campaign to finance the construction of its new building, such an intensive effort could not be sustained on a continuous basis. Endowments actually play a relatively small role in the school's fundraising strategy. As the dean noted, "I do not see us as a wonderful endowment target. We are not a hospital, church, halfway house, or basic science lab." Alumni support was another possibility, but as several professors explained, conventional wisdom holds that the bulk of alumni support is directed toward undergraduate institutions. While some professors believe that increasing loyalty to Anderson may yield substantial donations down the road, in the past and at present, such donations have been inadequate to meet its needs.

What Anderson needed was a sustained source of revenue to fund its growth. The most obvious solution was to raise tuition and fees. Soon after the arrival of a new dean in 1993, the school received permission from the university to add an additional fee onto the cost of the MBA program. This differential fee continued to rise over the years. By 1998, the annual out-of-state tuition for the MBA program was up to $20,000, bringing it in line with the tuition at comparable institutions (see Table 3.1).

Revenue from differential fees proved insufficient to maintain the building and compete in what professors call the big leagues. The dean explained:

> We are at a juncture where we compete with the top institutions across the country. We internally have to make some decisions about our resolve to compete and to secure an operating environment that allows us to do it. It's possible to do, but it's not easy. The differential fees that we have been allowed to charge have been instrumental in getting us to this point, but it's up to us to take command of what is going on and to create a financial future that will allow us to keep going.

Table 3.1

Annual Out-of-State Tuition for MBA Program at Selected Institutions

	1994	*1996*	*1998*
Harvard	$20,960	$23,840	$26,260
Stanford	$21,189	$23,100	$24,990
Pennsylvania	$21,050	$23,608	$24,990
Michigan	$20,960	$23,180	$23,840
UCLA	$14,496	$18,963	$20,093

Source: *Business Week Online* at http://bwnt.businessweek.com/faqsnfigs/index.asp

The School Responds

New Sources of Revenue

Part of the answer came from revenues provided by two non-traditional MBA programs: The Executive MBA (EMBA) program, which was established in 1982 and costs $28,000 per year, and the Fully Employed MBA (FEMBA) program, established in 1988, which costs $18,000 per year. Together, these two programs constituted more than one-quarter of Anderson's total revenues in 1997-1998. More recently, the school began to capitalize on its Executive Education Program, established in 1946 as a continuing education program for professionals. Executive Education quickly proved itself as an important source of revenue. An Anderson administrator explained:

> In the past, when we were almost fully funded by the state, the Executive Education Program was looked at like a little golden pot of money that the dean used for discretionary funding for professors who needed things, and to do things here and there. But now it's almost part of the operating budget.

Far from reaching its full potential, the Executive Education Program is expected to grow in importance. The dean predicted that even after the MBA's differential fees level off, fees from the Executive Education Program will keep climbing, making it the school's revenue leader. He explained UCLA's unique positioning in this area:

> Northwestern does $25 million a year in executive education. We do $3 million to $6 million. We have an advantage in that we don't split our geographic region with a major competing institution. Northwestern has Chicago to compete with, Berkeley has Stanford, and Harvard has MIT. Here we are, strategically located on the Pacific Rim with USC and us. East to Texas and north to Berkeley, there's nobody else. Clearly, there is growth potential there.

The trend toward executive education, however, is not without controversy. While no one disputes its potential as a source of revenue, some question whether it fits the school's traditional research and teaching mission. Many faculty members voice concern that the Executive Education Program compromises the school's research orientation, and dampens the research model. Because much of their teaching is elementary, little of their research is used. Some think the school is drifting closer to a model of corporate training, a path they believe could have serious negative consequences. One faculty member explained:

> We're doing things that don't necessarily, that aren't necessarily based strictly on our research. And we have to do them in order to maintain the quality of the institution as a whole. But it does lead us into areas where it's not entirely clear what our core competence is. And you know, once we start getting into some of these areas, we're competing with private consultants and corporate training programs and a variety of other things. It does raise some difficult issues about where we draw the line between the kinds

of programs and the kinds of things that we will do and the kinds of programs and the kinds of things that we won't do. It raises questions about the criteria we use in promoting our faculty, and this will ultimately lead to the dilution of our research orientation.

Because teaching in the Executive Education Program is so highly paid, it is considered a privilege. But professors question whether it is the wisest use of professors' time, especially given the competition among business schools. One explained:

We may be going a bit overboard in trying to expand the number of programs in the Executive Education Program. We'll have to see whether the faculty in the long run can deal with yet another drain on their resources. While it may generate funds, it may not be the most useful way to spend faculty time. It might be better at this point to have less money and to get the research out, especially since we're trying to bump our way up in the rankings right now.

Despite the controversy, there is no question that the FEMBA, EMBA, and Executive Education Program have substantially changed the financial profile of the school. Between 1986 and 1997, the proportion of Anderson's total revenue mostly attributable to these programs (included under sales and services) grew from 16% to more than 50%, helping raise total revenues from about $15 million in 1986 to almost $40 million in 1997 (see Table 3.2).

A Distinctive and Technologically Advanced New Building

In the early 1990s, the school began constructing a new building that the faculty and administration hoped would give Anderson a competitive edge. With the help of a $15 million donation from real estate tycoon John Anderson, the school embarked on a fundraising campaign and eventually raised

Table 3.2

Total Revenue and Percentage from Various Sources
for The Anderson School, 1986-1997

Source	1986	1987	1988	1989	1990	1991	1992	1993	1994	1995	1996	1997
Endowments	0.4	0.4	0.5	0.5	0.7	0.8	1.1	0.9	0.8	0.4	0.4	0.6
General Funds	61.9	59.9	61.1	59.1	55.2	52.6	48.1	9.2	45.7	25.0	38.0	32.7
Tuition & Fees	2.4	2.1	1.6	1.1	1.1	1.0	0.8	0.9	1.2	1.6	3.7	10.0
Special State Appropriations	2.1	1.6	1.6	1.5	1.4	1.6	1.5	1.1	0.7	0.4	0.6	0.2
Federal Grants & Contracts	2.3	1.7	1.3	1.5	1.0	2.9	3.7	2.9	1.6	0.9	1.3	0.9
Private Gifts, Contracts & Grants	14.5	16.8	15.1	12.6	13.2	11.4	12.3	10.5	8.5	9.8	8.2	5.4
Sales & Services	16.3	17.4	18.7	23.6	27.2	29.4	31.3	33.5	41.4	61.8	47.4	50.2
Other	0.1	0.1	0.1	0.1	0.1	0.3	1.2	0.9	0.2	0.1	0.3	0.1
Reserve	0.0	0.0	0.1	0.1	0.0	0.0	0.0	0.0	0.0	0.1	0.1	0.0
Total Revenue (in millions)	15.0	16.4	16.6	18.0	21.2	22.7	24.2	24.7	25.0	48.4	35.5	39.6

Source: *UCLA Corporate Finance Department, 1997*

almost $100 million dollars to finance the creation of a structure that today is described as the "most technologically advanced educational facility in the nation" (Anderson 1997 MBA Brochure).

Opened in 1995, the structure sits at the north end of the UCLA campus. Looking like a cross between the corporate headquarters of a Fortune 500 company and a library, the Anderson complex consists of seven distinct buildings linked by a series of bridges that connect the towers at various levels. The Romanesque-style structure is modeled after an Italian hillside community though one has to use a powerful imagination to make the connection. Several outdoor terraces hug the exterior of the building, providing expansive views of south campus. The interior of the building is designed in open landscape style, with natural light provided from skylights and atria. Inside the building, sweeping staircases wrap around glass-enclosed elevators.

The key selling point of the new building is its technology. Virtually all classrooms and meeting rooms have extensive audiovisual capabilities, including overhead projectors, recessed projection screens, teleconferencing capabilities, and satellite hookups. More than 2,500 network ports link every seat in the school's 78 classrooms—as well as many in the lounge and library—to the Internet, enabling students and professors to electronically communicate with each other and access the web. Students are required to purchase laptop computers upon enrolling in Anderson to ensure that the technology is used to its fullest capacity.

Unexpected Consequences

Increased Competition from Rankings

Despite everyone's hopes, the new building was not a panacea, a point driven home for many by the 1996 *Business Week* rankings. In 1988, Anderson had debuted in the rankings in 16th place. By 1994, the school had jumped to ninth place, a coveted spot placing it among the top ten business schools. In 1996, however, the school slipped back to 12th place. The drop was a surprise, especially given the new building. One professor said dejectedly, "We have this brand new facility… we thought it would pay off in terms of rankings."

Slipping to 12th place indicated something had gone wrong, and the bad news quickly became the focal point of discussion. A senior professor added:

> It is a signal that something is not quite what it should be. Our perception is that we should be at least among the top ten business schools in the country. But the ranking tells us we are not.

Many faculty members simply dismissed the rankings. Some criticized them because they failed to include any measures of research excellence or faculty productivity. One commented, "We can all be Nobel Prize winners and end up ranked the number 200th business school." Most of the criticism, however, centers on what is considered a flawed methodology. While ranking the universe of business schools is a valid way to show gross differences among the 700-plus business schools across the nation, critics claim it is an unreliable way to rank the top ten or 20. Anderson professors complain that this kind of ranking is not valid because, as one put it, "It is impossible for schools to fluctuate so wildly from year to year." Another elaborated:

> You can look at how the top ten schools change in the rankings from year to year and think of that as variance. Then you can think about whether the school could actually be changing in its quality that rapidly. The answer is "no". So you see, there is an enormous amount of noise.

Despite their criticisms, professors acknowledge that the rankings are a good barometer of how Anderson is perceived by students and the Fortune 500 companies, and as such, they cannot be taken lightly. As one professor observed, "The rankings are picking something up. Whether it's accurate or not is beside the point. In a marketplace, it's perception that counts." Ironically, when we disaggregated the rankings we found that the evaluations from company recruiters were dragging them down. In the 1988 ranking, Anderson came in first in the poll of graduates. But it was ranked 18th by company recruiters. Reasons that recruiters gave in interviews hint at the reasons. Some recruiters thought that Anderson students had too much theory and lacked practical application, while other expressed doubts that UCLA students would be willing to move away from the sunshine and the beach to the east coast.

The rankings appear to have little effect on the school's ability to recruit faculty because, according to the interim dean, professors being recruited consider other factors, such as the quality of their colleagues and their work. He explained:

> We've placed between nine and 16 since the rankings started. Any movement in that range will not have a significant impact on attracting faculty. Faculty tend to look most closely at who is there and what they are doing.

But rankings do affect the school's ability to attract top-notch students. One professor said, "The applicants feel that if they get into a highly ranked school, they'll have better job prospects and they may be able to earn a higher salary, or get a better career path. At least that is the perception."

In this case, there may be some truth to the perception. Professors say that some high-end consulting firms will only recruit from the top ten schools, and that when Anderson's rankings dropped to 12th, they stopped recruiting. This was especially disconcerting to the career placement staff. An administrator explained, "They worry that if Anderson is 20 or 15, rather than five, somehow their people aren't as marketable as the ones that are in the top five." The slippage does not sit well with students, who see their employment prospects dwindle. "When the top companies stopped coming," said one professor, "students became enormously agitated."

Making matters worse, faculty and administrators fear that the drop in ranking could also translate into a drop in revenue, since consulting firms will pay employees' tuition for programs offered at the top business schools. One professor explained:

> One of my best students—she got an A+ in my class—said that when she came here, she was at McKinsey, and they said that they normally only pay for tuition to the top schools. She said she wanted to go to UCLA—we were number 12 at the time—and they were reluctant to pay.

Faculty and administrators worry that there is a relationship between the school's ranking and the number of applicants.

While difficult to discern, the relationship between rank and volume of high quality applications is probably not imaginary. According to one tenured professor, applications to University of Chicago's business school were cut in half when the school slipped out of *Business Week's* top ten.

Shrinking PhD Program

As the MBA program grew, the PhD program shrank—from more than 100 graduate students in 1993 to approximately 60 in 1997. Professors offer a variety of reasons for the downsizing. Some point to a decline in the market demand for PhD graduates, which parallels a drop in business-school growth that peaked in the late 1980s. To avoid producing PhDs who can't be placed, the school has made a conscious effort to reduce supply. At the same time, professors say, the PhD applicant pool has weakened. One faculty member explained:

> Part of our obligation is to help our students find jobs. But now, the market is very tight. So unless the candidate is truly outstanding, it's not fair to them to invest that kind of duration to do a PhD and not be able to find a decent job.

Another reason for the shrinking PhD program, according to a substantial number of faculty members, is that it's too costly to maintain. Doctoral students typically are fully funded for at least the first few years of their program and are thus viewed as a drain on resources. One professor explained:

> The argument is made that there aren't any jobs and so on. But there actually are jobs; it's just that it's expensive to have these doctoral students around because they compete for resources with other hungry mouths.

The PhD program is especially difficult to maintain and support because it is so fundamentally different than the MBA. One professor explained:

Doctoral-level coursework is very disjointed from the MBA program. Doctoral students do take MBA courses, but they really need to have special doctoral courses. Our MBA program is professional. It's trying to produce practitioners, not academicians. The PhD program is designed to produce faculty. And the two don't overlap that much. That makes the PhD program very, very hard to support in a school that is basically funded by tuition, rather than research.

The decline in the PhD program troubles some professors, who believe that it threatens the long-term viability of the school. It is the PhD program, they say, that fulfills the research function of the institution. One professor explained:

The doctoral program is not high on the list for fresh resources because it's not seen as something that, in the short term, will bolster our revenue generating capacity. And in the short term it probably won't. But in the long run, if we don't have a vital research center to the school and a research orientation, which I think depends in part on having a thriving doctoral program, we're in a sense eating our seed corn.

Another faculty member predicted that should Anderson's emphasis on the doctoral program continue to decline, its credibility will come into question:

We've established ourselves as the premier research-oriented management school in Southern California. How can we profess to be a school based on research and yet have hardly any doctoral students? But if we continue to allocate resources [away from the doctoral program], we'll be a little more hucksterish.

Redefinition of Student as Customer

While it would have been unusual a decade ago to hear professors characterize students as customers, today it is not. At least two factors are behind this change in concept. One is the rising cost of the MBA program. "Students are paying more, so they want more," said one professor, echoing others. Another professor explained:

> We've raised tuition to the point that students now calculate how much each course costs, and they want to get their money's worth. They want to get what they pay for.

A third added:

> They're paying the market price for their MBA, and they think they deserve this kind of experience. They're saying, 'For what I'm paying, I expect to have a high-impact experience, not just get my ticket punched.'

As the MBA became a passport to high earnings and students were willing and able to pay high tuitions, they became redefined as customers. Business school rankings also were influential in forging this new concept—one that not all professors were eager to accept. One explained:

> The rankings clearly empowered the student as customer, not just student. At the beginning, many people just hoped it would go away. But it didn't. The rankings created a ground swell and started to gain momentum. As it did, it made teaching more important; it just raised the salience of teaching. It empowered the student as customer, not just as student. That changed some things.

MBA students are not shy about exercising their rights as customers. According to Anderson professors, today's students want a teaching experience that is more akin to entertainment than traditional education. Professors say their students want them to be enthusiastic, exciting, and dynamic. One elaborated:

> They want to know that every moment they are sitting there, their mind is going to be stimulated and they are going to think this is terrific and interesting and impactful. When that doesn't occur, rather than think it's normal or okay, or that maybe they as the student should integrate the material, they think the professor is not doing his or her job.

Rather than a standard lecture, students now expect multimedia presentations and well-orchestrated performances. When their expectations are not met, they let their dissatisfaction be known. One professor explained:

> They want everything choreographed so it's like walking into a play for the evening. They want the materials to be ready and to look all nice and neat and slick and everything to be laid out and planned. They want to have a set of bullet points on the Internet that they can look at when they hear a lecture. They pick on us about petty things, like whether your handouts are three-hole punched or not, or whether your overheads are in PowerPoint. And they want to have the current newspaper show up in class everyday in some unusual way. They want to see juggling and video clips, stuff like that. That's increased.

Professors also report that students display a decreasing tolerance for theory. One said, "The MBAs, they don't want to hear the 'r' word—research—forget it. Or the 'a' word—academics." Another added:

> Students are starting to come back and say the classes are too theoretical. That's interesting

because it's the same class—the level of theory I'm teaching is the same as six or seven years ago—but the students are reacting to it differently.

Still another grumbled:

In the MBA program, you can't possibly try to teach any of them complex mathematics. They don't want to learn it. That's what my students tell me. They just want to use Excel and solve an eight-by-eight program.

Professors complain that they spend so much time explaining how theories can be applied to students who they say have little tolerance for ambiguity. One said:

They want the content delivered in a way that the connection to their careers, to their potential roles as managers or consultants or traders on Wall Street or whatever it is they choose to do, is pretty darn immediately clear.

When professors decide to teach theory, they feel they have to justify their choice to students. One explained:

If you say, 'We're going to study demand curves' you need to explain to them the reason why. 'Because you need to be able to do forecasting, understand reservation prices, price elasticity, etc., all these things that are vitally important for you as a manager to understand.' You need to be constantly motivating and linking and justifying for them.

Tensions inevitably surface when professors feel that students' demands go too far. Some professors say they feel pressure to prove their worth to students unlike in the past, when students accepted professors' credibility as a given. Professors become particularly annoyed when they feel that students' demands for relevance disrupt learning. One used a joke to illustrate his point:

Here, the premise is that you have to prove to
them that you're worthwhile. I like to describe it
in terms of a joke in which the first-grade teacher
says, 'Two plus two equals four and I want everybody in this classroom to learn this.' And the kid
in the back of the class raises his hand and says,
'Can you give me a business example of that?'
That's typical of MBA training. They're not going
to believe that two plus two equals four is useful
to know. The teacher has to convince them that
that's useful knowledge. That affects the way the
classroom operates. You spend a tremendous
amount of energy at the beginning of and end of
class proving or demonstrating that two plus two
equals four is a good thing to know.

Most professors express dismay at students' superficial
motives. "Most just want a stamp on the forehead for the least
amount of work possible," one complained. He continued, "The
faculty are upset that we have a culture of students who live
here two years in (upscale) Manhattan Beach and do as little
work as possible and then get a big salary increase." Veteran
faculty members recall that in the past students wanted to learn.
One lamented:

Students used to struggle with the questions that
you posed to them. Today they say, 'Well, you
haven't made it clear. How do I get an A?' And
you say to them, 'Well, the subject matter isn't
clear. That's the whole point.' And they'll say,
'Well then, why don't you teach us something
that is clear?' They are less committed to the
notion of management as a profession, more
committed to getting the degree and getting out.

Ironically, most lay the problem at the feet of marketplace
economics. There is general agreement that few students are
seeking intrinsic rewards from the MBA but rather a ticket to

advance their own careers or to get a raise. According to one professor:

> With the MBA they became more oriented to this paper degree. It's like selling soap, like you're Proctor and Gamble. They don't care about actually doing anything to actually improve the company. The whole objective is to get their piece of paper so they can get a raise. And the whole point of the school is not to teach them anything. Nobody cares about learning anything.

Over time, faculty members complain, students' money-driven motives rub off on them, making them cynical about teaching in the MBA program. One said:

> To me what you have is a tremendous cynicism that has developed about the MBA where there's this complete severance from any intellectual pursuit. Nobody really gives a damn whether the students or the faculty, whether they're learning, as long as they get the piece of paper. Go and interview the students. They'll tell you they came here to get this piece of paper so they can get a raise. They're not coming here to learn anything about the history of the Western civilization, the rise of mathematics, or the import of optimization. It's a joke. Everybody's cynical about the whole damn thing.

Not surprisingly, resentment among the faculty is on the rise. Some professors say they have little regard for students' demands, especially when they are loafing. One professor explained:

> The problem is that they're not willing to put forth the effort. I would be perfectly happy to spend a lot of time with them if they were willing to actually do their part of the bargain, but

they're not doing that. So we have to do things like grade-school stuff—make them hand in weekly homework, disconnect the Network during class so they can't send email back and forth or call up the Playboy page. It's somewhat childish behavior.

One professor recalled an interaction with a student that was astonishing. He said in amazement:

> I had a student who said, 'Look, I'm a busy person. I need to be spoon-fed.' He actually used the word spoon-fed! . . . This current crop of students is the most vindictive bunch of little turkeys I've ever met—very vicious little blood-sucking leeches. They're demanding everything.

Renewed Emphasis on Teaching

Despite the pernicious effects of student having become redefined as customer, a growing number of professors acknowledge that the shift has ultimately had a positive effect on the quality of teaching. As business schools sought to raise their status in the academic community, theoretically driven research began to dominate. Some faculty members agree that the field had become too esoteric and that the national rankings may have provided accurate feedback that made the pendulum swing back. One faculty member explained:

> In the 1950s and 1960s, management education was generally considered a trade school that was very relevant to business but not very academically rigorous. In the 1970s and 1980s, a whole new generation of faculty was trained in hard sciences, such as statistics and econometrics and mathematics, so the academic level rose. But into the 1970s and 80s, we became a bit too esoteric and lost touch a little. Fortunately, our audience, which is basically corporate America, through

the *Business Week* surveys, punish those who only
do the esoteric material and don't teach a really
good managerial program. So now we're being
held accountable for two audiences. We have to
be academically rigorous, but we also have to be
relevant.

Teaching has become much more important in management
schools than it was 20 years ago, a trend again at least partially
attributable to the rankings. One professor explained:

A huge shift, one that really impacts our lives, is
that teaching has become much more important
in a management school than it was 20 years ago.
Good or bad, the fact is that the *Business Week* ratings have a lot of influence. A big part of the rat-
ing is student satisfaction and the quality of
teaching. So at UCLA, if you talk to people
who've been here a long time, they will tell you
that the emphasis on teaching is probably the single biggest change in the profession in the last 20
years.

Some professors acknowledge that improvements in the
quality of teaching were needed. One noted:

It's true that all our faculty used to say, 'I don't
give a rat's ass what the students think.' They
didn't put their syllabi together, were very unor-
ganized, and didn't think about how to put the
material together in any kind of interesting or
coherent way. But by God, we just can't put up
with that anymore. So that's a positive [outcome].

Improving the quality of teaching was considered so important that in 1995, the school hired a consultant to coach professors how to be more effective in class. The consultant used theater as a metaphor for the classroom, where the instructor was
the director. Though using her services was voluntary, half of

the Anderson professors signed up. While there was some skepticism at first, the majority said they found the workshops useful. One professor remembered:

> She would give you pointers on what you could do better. Raise your voice level, or become more energetic. I, for instance, use a lot of handouts and look for some discussion among the students in the courses to the extent that it is appropriate. I would basically stand close to the lectern, going over the handouts. She gave me some hints in terms of becoming a bit more animated. I found it very helpful.

The renewed focus on teaching means professors must spend more time than ever before preparing. One explained:

> Ten years ago, assuming you knew your subject, you could just go in and talk. You didn't have to spend very much time preparing. Now, I spend much more time preparing materials, cases for discussion, updating, etc. It's not a matter of just going in and talking. So there's more work involved.

Another said, "I have to spend a third more time in the preparation, even on a course I've taught 17 times before. I spend a third more time on the prep, and I get lower teacher ratings."

Professors generally admire and appreciate the school's new building and its technological capabilities. In the classroom, the Intranet (Anderson's internal electronic network that is closed to the general public) enables professors to access and alter students' work in real time for everyone to see. One professor enthusiastically explained:

> The effect of that on what happens in the classroom, particularly in the more analytically oriented courses, is just phenomenal to see. An instruc-

tor can have any student put up on the screen, from his or her seat in the class, some analysis that that student has done. Maybe it's part of their case analysis or some other analytical exercise like a financial analysis. It becomes a very dynamic process in ways that just weren't possible before. You might start with a particular response that some student has done in preparation for the class. But you don't have to stop there – you're not stuck with what people have done in preparation. You can change it online during the conversation. You can change variables, you can change assumptions, you can compare that to somebody else's at the same time, right up there on the screen!

Professors and students also have direct access to the web, since every seat in every classroom is hard-wired to the Internet. The effect, as another professor explained, is "the ability to go seamlessly between a presentation that I'm making on PowerPoint, Excel spreadsheets that the students prepared, gathering information about a company on the web, and the VCR, all in one seamless presentation." As a result, he said, "I think the students appreciate that, and I think I can get them to learn a little more than I would have been able to otherwise."

Laptops and the Intranet also have enabled electronic communication, which some professors say has made it possible to utilize time between classes more effectively. One professor explained how he uses technology to bridge the gap between the Executive MBA classes, which sometimes meet only once every two weeks. He said:

Usually, time between classes is like dead silence. So I use email in the interim to continue the conversations that we had in the classroom. I can point them to an article I just read in the *Wall Street Journal* and say this is what we talked about in the classroom last week, or two weeks ago, etc.

So it's not exactly a feedback situation, but you get them involved in the thinking in the dead time between classrooms.

Technology also has decreased the need for office hours because many professors do their student counseling electronically or on the phone. One professor said:

I've found that 90% of the questions that students have can be answered electronically very easily. So you provide a good service for your students. Of course if it's a serious problem, they come in. But [with email], they don't need to sit here and waste your time and their time with a physical trip to the office. Because of that, more time is freed up for other activities.

On the other hand, the advances in technology have had some unanticipated and surprising costs and drawbacks, some of which may work themselves out in time. Several professors said they are just now learning how to use the technology effectively, and that it will be another three to five years before they truly use laptop computers pedagogically. The Anderson School librarian said:

One of the biggest challenges is to integrate technology into what goes on around here so the students don't feel like they're carrying around laptops that are nothing more than expensive paperweights.

Taking advantage of the Internet requires faculty members to spend considerable amounts of time redesigning their syllabi, creating web pages, and uploading slides. Some express resentment over this added work, especially when they feel they are rewarded more for research than teaching. Others note that excessive use of PowerPoint slides and presentations create too passive an environment for students to internalize material and actually learn.

But professors complain that students use their laptops for entertainment or other purposes during class rather than for learning. The way classrooms are set up exacerbates the problem. Because students face the professor, the professor cannot see the students' computer screens. One professor said:

> With the onset of technology, there's been a disastrous change in the classroom climate. Students sit there with laptops open on their desks, plugged into the network. If you sit in the back of the room, you see they're watching Pointcast, web-browsing, doing their email, or their finance homework. The PointCast technology is noxious because it's a screen saver, so if you're not doing anything it comes up. It sucks data off the web and presents it in sort of a visual animated format. So a student can honestly say, 'I'm not using the computer.' But it's sitting there like a movie, feeding them *CNN*, the front page of the *L.A. Times*, the *Wall Street Journal*, stock prices, all this stuff going on, while you're trying to teach a class! And they're watching the tube! Noxious!

One professor who sat in the back of the room one day was amazed to observe students' inattention and poor manners. He said:

> I was watching a guy buying a Jag in the back of the classroom—scanning car statistics, Jags, BMWs and Mercedes, that sort of thing. Somebody else was reading today's edition of the *Cambodian Times*. Another guy was logged onto the Playboy web page. So there's been a lot of flaming stuff going back and forth. I had a Nokia client who wanted to do an international field study sitting in, and about five students had Playmates on their screens. He essentially ignored that.

While the logical solution might be to ask students to turn off their computers, this in essence defeats the purpose of technology-ready facilities and would be highly unpopular among students. One professor said:

> If you were to turn to your class and say, 'I want these computers turned off, we're having a discussion here,' you'd hear howls of protest, your teaching evaluations would go into the toilet, and the dean would hear about it. That's the social tension we're under here.

While the school had responded quickly to increased competition, rankings, and the need for new sources of revenue, it discovered that its actions produced some serious unintended consequences. Considering the students "customers" and tipping the balance, especially in a research university, toward teaching, had for the senior faculty gone too far.

The School Corrects

By 1997, most professors agreed that the student as customer had gone too far and had led to a decline in academic rigor. One professor remembered thinking:

> We have to make some fundamental improvements in our MBA program to make it more academically rigorous. It has been corrupted to a substantial extent by the tyranny of the teaching evaluation by MBA students.

As an administrator explained, the pendulum began to swing back:

> This trend toward dumbing-down courses had reached an extreme. The pendulum is now swinging back. Faculty members want to have a high-quality product that gives the MBA students practical training, but it's not an on-the-job train-

ing program. It comes from a research institution, and they want this curriculum to reflect that.

An interdisciplinary MBA task force began meeting weekly to investigate how to restructure the MBA program. One decision was to standardize core courses and examinations. The core, as it is known, is a series of about seven required, first-year courses that serve as the basis for second-year courses. In past years, professors taught a similar set of topics in the core courses, but they had a great deal of latitude and created their own exams. In the early 1990s, according to one professor, "anybody could do basically what he or she wanted, even in a core class." As a result, professors sometimes had difficulty linking their class material to core classes. As one professor explained, "When you say to students, 'As you saw in your finance class' or whatever, half of them nod 'yes' and half nod 'no'."

Today, professors teaching core classes collectively determine topics, and share common syllabi, common readings, and a common examination. One result, professors say, is that they have begun to redefine their roles as coaches helping students get over a common bar. Having common examinations also eliminates pressures for professors to dumb down courses to get high student evaluation scores. One professor explained:

> We're saying to the students that instructors have no choice [about what was on the test], this was going to be one common exam. It wasn't the instructor that was forcing this hard stuff on them, it was this autonomous, common exam. And so we were there to help them prepare, we were forced to go through this hard stuff even though we might not even agree that it should be taught. So we were their buddy!

Not surprisingly, some professors consider common examinations as bars to their creativity. But, despite any loss of creativity, most faculty members view standardization as inevitable. One said:

In some ways, having a common exam is a basic violation of UC rules. But if you don't do that, then the students get all up in arms and say, 'They got A's, and did the same kind of work that I got a C for' or, 'You spent too much time on your own stupid stuff and didn't give us the good stuff.' It's a market. You can only be autonomous for so long until the chain gets jerked.

The Double Bind of Research and Teaching

It is no secret that unless professors publish research results in what are considered high-quality journals, they put their careers at peril—especially those who lack the security of tenure. Professors speak realistically and unemotionally about the publish or perish phenomenon. They acknowledge that despite the great emphasis on teaching, there is no way our research isn't going to be anything but number one. Professors are expected to publish at least two articles each year in refereed journals. But the increased emphasis on teaching, with no let-up on pressure for research, leads many professors to say they feel caught in a double bind. One professor said:

> The emphasis on research is something that is going to be tough to sustain in the environment where we have constituencies demanding more of us to spend more time on things that are not going to lead to journal articles.

The focus on teaching has increased the importance of non-ladder faculty members, lecturers, and adjunct professors whose sole responsibility is teaching. Lecturers and adjuncts are valued for their real-world experience and for their dedicated student-as-customer focus. One professor explained:

> The adjunct non-ladder faculty... often times are the people who have the real-world experience, who have the contacts, who understand how to deliver a product—a teaching product or some

other kind of partnership product—to someone in the private sector.

The role of adjuncts was in the spotlight after *Business Week* named two Anderson adjunct professors among the top five adjunct professors in the nation. But the recognition also created a dilemma for regular professors who must do research but are also held to the same high teaching standards as adjuncts. One said:

> The incentive structure is such that if you don't do the research, you're going to lose your job. So you have to think, well, I could spend, you know, an extra eight hours making this class absolutely top notch or I could spend eight hours doing something else and leave the class as being pretty decent. And that trade-off depends on the individual. And the adjunct's teaching is absolutely outstanding, so it makes it harder for the rest of us. [Laughter] You know we have some professors here who after every class will send an individualized email to every student in the classroom reporting on his or her performance. I mean that's the extent of customer service that some of the students can get.

Assistant professors feel the dilemma especially acutely, some professors say, because they expend a lot of energy on work that doesn't always matter in the classroom. One tenured professor explained:

> The great adjunct professor gets the teaching awards. Well now how do you think assistant professors feel? They're supposed to come in here and be academic and crank out research papers and yet that whole side of them isn't allowed to show in the classroom. Well, they're disenfranchised.

The expectation that new faculty members must also be stellar teachers to get promoted is relatively new and signals a change in the school's culture. It has also raised the bar for new faculty members. One professor explained:

> At least for junior faculty, those good ratings are needed for the promotion system. But it establishes a Zeitgeist in which that level of teaching evaluation is expected for what would be considered acceptable performance in general.

Finding such a combination of research and teaching talent, however, is not easy, as one professor explained:

> We are becoming so picky; hardly anybody cuts the mustard anymore. It is unbelievable how demanding we are. We want people to be absolutely top flight, scholar-wise. And we want them to be really dynamic and engaging in the classroom. That's a totally different skill set. Good researchers tend to have a certain personality type, and now we need people who are sort of gregarious and have certain teaching abilities. So few people meet that criterion.

Privatization

It is obvious that the Anderson School is on a course toward privatization. As part of a seemingly never-ending search for additional funds, the school has embarked on a major development and alumni relations campaign to attract new revenue sources. One professor put the trend in a historical context:

> Many of the issues that face Anderson, and even the university, today stem from pressures that universities historically were sheltered from, either because they were private and students paid entirely for their own way and/or there were endowments. Or they were public, and

there was rest-assured revenue from the government. But that's changed. Private universities feel
it as well, because they can't cover their costs in
today's environment through traditional tuition
costs, research grant costs, and endowment.

Despite the fact of its being part of a public university, the
Anderson School has tried to distinguish itself as a semi-pri-
vate, autonomous professional school. Renaming itself the
Anderson School followed the lead of other top business
schools like Wharton and Kellogg that have established themselves as separate institutions rather than as part of the universities they inhabit.

The shift toward privatization is not without controversy.
Becoming market-driven and separate from the larger university has, some feel, led faculty members away from their core
competency and from the priorities of a research institution.
One professor explained:

The need to raise money used to be on the bottom. Controlling our own fate is driving us to
activities that consume a lot of time and are not
amenable to this being a place where you do
research and, by the way, teach, which is where I
think the priorities ought to be.

The perceived loss of rigor in the MBA program, coupled
with the decline in the PhD program and growth of the
Executive Education Program, have led an increasing number
of professors to express concern that market forces are leading
the school away from its core competence: research. The growing schism between teaching and research in philosophies,
according to a number of professors, is producing two camps—
those who do research, and those who teach. Because of the
growing number of adjuncts and lecturers who specialize in
teaching, some feel that the faculty is in danger of becoming
polarized into a research camp that can't teach, and a teaching
camp that has no academic credibility. One professor explained:

Basic research is often extremely technical and may have applications that take years to be realized. The same is true for the applied end. The people who do the consulting don't have time to do this kind of stuff. They're trying to figure out what the market trends are, sit with the stakeholders, spend the time, figure out where the intersections are, and trying to ride the wave of wherever intersections are and how it changes over time.

Some professors speak of the difficulty of trying to balance the market orientation with the preservation of a research mission. One explained:

As we stray further and further away from our core competence, which I think is our research and our scholarship, we essentially risk betraying our mission. On the other hand, we're stuck between a rock and a hard place, so we have to do the best we can in managing and always doing things that as much as possible are based on our core competence. I see that as about the most difficult issue that universities and professional schools face.

Need for a New Vision

Tired of feeling buffeted by market forces, many faculty members talk about the need for the school to establish a vision of what it wants to be. Some professors maintain that rather than try to be everything to everybody, the school should develop an identity, or find a niche in which it can excel. One explained:

People think some major change is necessary in order to establish an identity. We have tried to do too many things for a very broad range of constituencies, to be everything to everyone. With 1,000 students here at any one time, of course, there is a lot of emphasis on teaching, emphasis on satisfying some lowest common denominator.

Another, echoing a similar sentiment, said Anderson must differentiate itself from other business schools:

We cannot be the best at everything. We need to decide what our strength is and what we want to deliver. What's our product? What are our advantages, and what niche can we fill? Should we just continue with everybody else in the nation, or is there something that defines us, that's our characteristic, that's different from others?

Differentiation among business schools is an inevitable trend, say some professors. One explained:

Schools looking at competitive strategies are trying to find their own competitive niche. The one thing you can guarantee is that they're going to be different rather than all fighting to operate with the same number.

An administrator elaborated, saying that only elite institutions with long histories can successfully follow a generalist strategy:

Our biggest challenge is to figure out what we really want to be excellent at. I don't think we really have a niche. I think we could have a couple of niches—international business in the Pacific Rim or entrepreneurialism. Those kinds of things could really be our areas to shine. But for whatever reason, we have not really capitalized on that. Unless you're a Harvard or somebody that has a several-hundred-year-old reputation, you have to have something that really sets you apart. You can't be everything to everybody.

Other professors think that the school needs to consider more seriously what it does well and build the MBA program around it, rather than the other way around. Yet others argue that Anderson should follow in the footsteps of the California Institute of Technology. A proponent of this idea explained:

> My vision is for [Anderson] to become the Caltech of business schools. Caltech is known for the greatest physics—every physics student wishes he were there. It is very specialized.

Becoming more of a Caltech would mean, according to one professor, downsizing the number of students, reducing the number of MBA programs, increasing the emphasis on research and integrating it more into teaching, and decreasing the growing emphasis on executive education and non-degree programs.

Not all professors agree with this idea. Some point out that becoming specialized is a dangerous move because it could be interpreted as a sign of weakness. One professor explained this point of view:

> If you look at the landscape of management schools around the country, I'd say the top 20— those who think of themselves as being in the top ten—typically don't specialize. If you read their mission statement, how they describe themselves, they like to think of themselves as full-service management schools, like Harvard. They think of themselves as an across-the-board, high-quality institution covering all aspects of management. Below that group, you see niche specialization. Babson College calls itself the entrepreneurial school. The business school at Sonoma State calls itself the wine business school. Thunderbird in Arizona calls itself the international business school. But among the top players, there is not much specialization. Management is a synthesis. People want to think of themselves as generalists. It would be less appealing if

students thought there was an aspect we didn't cover. We don't want to say that any one of our departments is less than stellar.

Others suggest that becoming specialized would result in a reduction in revenue, a prospect that the university administration would not welcome. Others point out that focusing on a certain area would be difficult given the multidisciplinary nature of the school. As one professor pointed out:

> [The Caltech] idea came from somebody quantitative, from finance or management science. But people who are in other areas probably would feel we shouldn't do that because that would mean we are going to be very technical and use computers and things like that. And not everybody here accepts that view. That's the problem. We have different people. In a business school there are different disciplines, from mathematics to economics to psychology, and therefore we have different backgrounds.

No matter which direction the school takes, everyone acknowledges it will take time. UCLA is a large bureaucracy and its traditions of shared governance ensure that change will be slow. One professor explained:

> Everybody is struggling with it. We're having lots of meetings about it. Everybody's got a different point of view and perspective that it's hard to get consensus on the next best thing to do. It's a collegial organization filled with people who have lifetime employment guarantees. You don't have the CEO saying, 'This is the strategy, this is what we're going to do.' Everything has to come from coalitions, and change is very slow. There is enormous inertia because you know the ship isn't going to sink tomorrow; it's going to sink slowly over the next 20 years.

But nearly everyone agrees that the school should stop paying so much attention to the *Business Week* rankings and focus on the long-term. A professor explained:

> We ought to do what we can do and do it well and let the rankings fall the way they fall. As soon as you start reacting to every little change in the way the winds blow, you're doomed to be blown every which way. I choke down nausea every time I see one of these things. 'Oh, the latest ranking is out. The sky is falling.' If we just worked more on building long-term strength, I think we'd be a lot better off.

Summary

Faculty

Faculty members in the Anderson School come from a variety of academic backgrounds including such diverse fields as economics, chemistry, engineering, and psychology. Like their counterparts in other departments, they found their way into the academic world both because they were committed to their research and because of the autonomy the career affords. In general, most are happy with their choice, despite the knowledge that they could earn higher salaries outside the university. A substantial number of professors say they conduct outside consulting to earn extra income and keep current in their fields.

Anderson professors work nearly ten hours each day, with the majority of their time divided almost equally between teaching and research. Reflecting the business world, they keep surprisingly regular, 9:00 to 5:00, hours on campus but often work longer hours into the evenings and weekends at home.

Much of the research conducted by Anderson faculty members is based on secondary data, including statistical model building and computer simulations, and it requires little in the way of external funding. As in other departments, to be promoted to a tenured position, professors must publish results of their work in what are regarded as top-tier scholarly journals.

While many faculty members were drawn to the university to conduct research, many say they now find that teaching takes a dominant portion of their time. Teaching in the MBA program requires considerable advance preparation, and it incorporates a surprising array of technology, from PowerPoint presentations to real time Internet research. Teaching in the Anderson School is driven by the student market. Upon graduation, Anderson students with MBAs are recruited intensively by top companies and they enjoy high starting salaries.

Pressures

As this case shows, growing pressures to become market driven are having a profound effect on the Anderson School. Two significant forces of change that have occurred within the last decade include the emergence of national rankings published by *Business Week* which, despite its controversial survey methodology, redefined students and employers as business school customers. These rankings have further intensified competition among business schools to be included in the top ten. Second, reductions in public funding have forced the school to offer new income-generating programs that lie beyond the scope of the school's research mission.

Changes

The resulting changes have not come without a cost. Faculty members worry that the rapid growth of the Executive Education Program coupled with the shrinkage of the PhD program is compromising the school's research mission and core competence. Spending more time than ever preparing for classroom teaching, many professors feel overworked and overloaded—and believe that the expectation to be both exceptional teachers as well as researchers is unrealistic. Many are dismayed at what they call the tyranny of student evaluations, which has led some professors to water down courses to prevent student dissatisfaction. Professors are troubled by the changes they perceive in the motives of MBA students, who some view as overly demanding and lacking intellectual curiosity. Finally, they voice concern at the growing reliance on adjunct professors, which has led some to predict that the school will bifurcate into two camps—a research camp that is not equipped to teach, and a teaching camp that lacks academic credibility.

Tired of feeling buffeted by these forces, professors feel the school should establish a new vision of what it wants to be. Meeting informally on a weekly basis, the faculty began debating two possible paths. Some believe the school should maintain its generalist strategy because they believe that specializing is a sign of weakness. Others believe the school should develop a niche because differentiation is an inevitable trend as competition among the top schools intensifies. The single issue that unites the faculty is the conviction that the school administration should pay less attention to the national rankings.

Addendum: From Late 1998 to 2001

A new dean was hired from the banking industry in mid-1999, and he moved quickly to establish task forces to help solve some of the school's more vexing problems. Despite the effort, many of the same issues that faced Anderson at the close of the study still persist. For instance, to continue to increase revenue, enrollments in the Fully-Employed MBA program (FEMBA) were increased 50% by adding a third section in the fall of 2000. The increase in enrollments has meant that when added to the Executive MBA students (EMBA) this group of about 680 students now exceeds the full-time MBA student population of about 640. Increasing enrollments of these nontraditional MBA students, some faculty worry, will alter the cohesive MBA student culture, increase the teaching load of ladder faculty, and dilute the quality of fully employed MBA students.

In 1998, the school was again ranked 12th by *Business Week* magazine, although there were signs that the faculty had become less willing to tolerate the consequences of taking the student as customer concept too far. As a result of one task force, a new student evaluation form was produced that asked fewer questions about faculty members' presentation styles and more about content and what students actually learned. The decision was also made not to include the anonymous forms in faculty records, where they could affect faculty members' promotion and tenure decisions. Currently discussions are underway to restrict, or to eliminate altogether, the use of student evaluations in core courses. Steps are being taken to reduce the decline in rigor and reverse the trend toward grade inflation by putting more stringent grading guidelines into place. A general guideline was also established that all core (required) MBA courses be taught by ladder faculty, rather than adjunct or visiting professors.

The student as customer philosophy continues, as evidenced by a number of curricular changes. In January 2000, keeping up with a trend set by other schools including Stanford, UC Berkeley, MIT, and Carnegie-Mellon, the school announced a new Center for Management in the Information Economy to meet students' demand for courses in e-commerce. Also, a new second-year elective track is being organized in the area of high technology management that will focus on issues related to the information economy, e-commerce, and management in technology based sectors. Finally, responding to the perception that new students' enthusiasm was being dulled by specialized courses early in their programs, the faculty has introduced more stimulating strategy courses earlier in the sequence.

4

The Graduate School of Education and Information Studies

The Graduate School of Education and Information Studies (GSE&IS) includes two academic departments—education and information studies. Both had been independent graduate schools for many years until 1994, when a university cost-savings initiative merged the two into a single graduate school. In 1998 the annual budget of the new school was about $27 million, placing it fifth in size among UCLA's nine professional schools.

Education

The Department of Education is housed in historic Moore Hall, one of UCLA's five original buildings constructed in 1930. The building was named after Los Angeles School Superintendent Ernest Carroll Moore, who was also UCLA's first provost. The education department enrolls about 800 graduate students each year and counts 47 full-time ladder faculty, 40 adjunct (or non-ladder) faculty, and 497 administrative staff as employees.

Students in the education department are concentrated in doctoral studies and masters degree teacher training—with a growing number in the undergraduate minor program. The department's academic programs are organized within five divisions: Higher Education and Organizational Change, Psychological Studies in Education, Social Research Methodology, Social Sciences and Comparative Education, and Urban Schooling. The Teacher Education Program (TEP) is housed within one of the school's research centers, known as Center X. The doctoral Educational Leadership Program cuts across the five divisions in matrix form. The school is also host to an on-campus laboratory elementary school and four other research centers.

One professor described the department as it was prior to the merger in the following way:

> The School of Education is like a quilt. In Spanish we say *cobija*. When you get under the quilt it means you are in *cobihado*. The school is a big tent. You have people working in psychology. That couldn't be further removed from my interests. You have people working in higher education. That overlaps somewhat with what I do... curriculum and instruction... research methods... So schools of education have all these disparate groups of people working on disparate subjects, and it's very difficult to figure out if there is a core that everybody should be exposed to. I'm not so sure there is one though there are different canons.

Information Studies

The Department of Information Studies (IS) is housed in a nondescript, three-story white office building located on the north side of the campus about 100 yards northeast of the Anderson School complex and about a ten minute walk from Moore Hall. IS offers specialties in information access, organization, systems and policy, and archives and preservation management. Twenty-two students are enrolled in doctoral studies while 121 are taking courses for master's degrees. The department employs 14 full-time ladder faculty members, and adjunct (or non-ladder) faculty, and 15 administrative staff.

Academic Life

While some faculty members complain about the pressures of research and teaching on their limited time, and others in IS grumble about the merger and their loss of status, most agree that the quality of life in the school is high. Faculty members socialize with each other in the hallways and in the mailroom (hall-talk is the chief form of informal communication that includes everything from chit-chat and gossip to more serious discussions about personnel and the school's finances). Friends of long standing often eat lunch with each other at the faculty center or have coffee together at the Kerckhoff coffeehouse located just west of Moore Hall. Many faculty and staff members have friendships with each other that extend beyond the campus and into their social lives. Unlike some other academic units where personal hostilities exist among professors, GSE&IS is remarkably free of personal antagonisms. Where they do exist, they are most often the result of conflict over personnel actions.

According to the memories of many senior faculty members, the general sense of goodwill and cooperation that today characterizes the school has fully emerged only in the last decade. A few veteran faculty members remember how UCLA Chancellor Franklin Murphy arrived in the early 1960s just as political power was shifting to the federal government and the federal government was spending record sums on research. Murphy, a medical doctor who would go on to become publisher of the *Los Angeles Times*, pressed what was then the Graduate School of Education to shift its focus from educational practice to research—a policy that produced conflict that has persisted for years. One education faculty member recalled:

> In the 1950s the power was in the office of teacher training. It had all the money and all the students. There were maybe 20 doctoral students in the school, but there were about 800 students training to become teachers. The whole second floor was an employment agency—a hub of constant activity. The dean's office was a little cubbyhole, but teacher training was huge.

Under Murphy, Howard Wilson, Dean of Education, began to rebuild the school in the image of the respected University of Chicago's School of Education. He proclaimed it would become a model of educational research, the Chicago of the West as he called it. At about the same time in 1960, California's first master plan for higher education reduced teacher training at the University of California, placing it in the California State University system. The master plan also had the effect of clarifying roles among the community colleges, the California State University system, and the University of California, that was solely charged with conducting research.

Many faculty members who had been hired in the 1960s and the early 1970s came from disciplines including psychology, sociology and statistics. They were recruited because of their backgrounds as researchers and, unlike their older colleagues, they were comfortable with the requirement to publish their research findings in peer-reviewed academic journals. A retired faculty member recalled the clash between the two camps:

> These people couldn't get jobs in their own disciplines so they came to us. They were always disgruntled because they hadn't been chosen for their own disciplines and they weren't educators. All you had to do was look in their mailboxes and you'd see psychology and sociology journals— nothing on education!

Another veteran faculty member recalled the shift to theoretical research vividly. He said:

> It was like night and day. These new faculty members spoke a different language than the oldtimers who had been hired in the 1930s and 1940s to train teachers and to work with the schools. The new researchers took on a higher status and it led to conflict between the two camps, especially when it came to issues of recruitment and promotion.

John I. Goodlad, a classroom teacher who had been educated at the University of Chicago, took over as dean in 1960 and led the former Graduate School of Education on an unprecedented rise as a research enterprise. Goodlad shrank teacher training into a small unit, greatly expanded doctoral training, and encouraged faculty members to seek outside funding for their research.

By the late 1980s, after many of the older faculty members had retired, educational research became the primary mission of the school and conflict began to subside. Yet the relationship between research and practice remained ill defined.

In 1992, an educational historian who had been a high-level administrator at Stanford University was appointed as dean. He arrived just as UCLA was struggling to adjust to a $110 million budget deficit. He was clear in his hopes to use the financial crisis to help the school strike a stronger balance between research and practice by refocusing the school's resources to improve educational practice. The dean commented that as a public institution, UCLA had a different responsibility to the state than did private universities:

> People look at us and ask, 'Why aren't you fixing the schools?' The reality is that much of what we do here is irrelevant to the improvement of schools, and that needs to change.

One senior faculty member echoed the same view and at a faculty meeting implored the faculty to rethink the connection between research and practice:

> The world of practice is a great opportunity for research questions. We're not asking for people to give up research but to lift their heads and move two steps over to a lush new pasture. There is a new market for work that crosses boundaries between research and practice.

Much of the faculty research failed to affect the practice of education because of the way faculty members are insulated from the external environment. He explained:

> The university's incentive systems have socialized generations of researchers. They tend to be unresponsive to demands that originate from

outside university boundaries. Customers of our research are the editorial boards of research journals. That creates a problem because research that's done to satisfy academic editorial boards is usually not applicable to the real world.

Faculty Autonomy and Entrepreneurialism

Even beginning assistant professors have wide discretion in what they choose to study and teach. Once advanced to a tenured position, professors' autonomy becomes nearly absolute, assuring them freedom to conduct research governed only by their interests or external funding with which to support it. For most, unfettered freedom is the most appealing aspect of an academic life. One faculty member explained:

> Few people have an opportunity to be in an environment in which they can speak freely, write freely, and share their world view with others without the fear of reprisal…

Another added:

> I don't particularly care about the formal institutional consent of what is right, what is appropriate, or what is needed, or what I should do in terms of my research agenda. I care about my own gut feelings about what needs to be said when and how. That's my privilege.

Finding the financial resources to support faculty research is time-consuming. Though *entrepreneur* is sometimes used privately to denigrate faculty members who seem motivated more by money than ideas, *entrepreneurialism* is a fact of life for faculty members who conduct large research projects. While some professors are supported through GSE&IS research centers, which are themselves sustained largely on soft money, most take responsibility for raising their own research funds from foundations and government agencies. A professor from information studies elaborated:

Getting research funds means being out there on the front lines. We are number one, the most scholarly ranking in the country... To keep that going you can't stand still. Academe is changing. Entrepreneurship, the expectation of bringing in your own money and supporting yourself – it's always been there in the sciences... I came out of a program with that ethic. You hit the ground running, getting grants from my first term as an assistant professor, 'cause that's how you got your research.

Service and Teaching

The dean said that when he arrived at UCLA he was impressed with the faculty's commitment to public service. He added:

People in the school have a sense of a calling apart from a cash orientation. There's the possibility of appealing to a higher ideal. They have a service orientation. They want their work lives to benefit others. Those who do research think the world will be better off because of what they are doing.

Indeed, a generally altruistic value orientation permeates the school. One education professor explained:

Even if they don't pay me anything, if they tell me, 'I'll pay you for your rent' and they give me money for my food. Even if I won the lottery tomorrow, if I won $10 million, I would probably be doing the same thing. Other activities would bore me. This gives me some happiness.

Another faculty member elaborated on rewards she has found in working with students. When asked if she felt fairly compensated by the university for her work she exclaimed, laughing and shaking her head:

> You mean money-wise? No! Money-wise I'm not.
> I'm recognized by my colleagues, and I feel vali-
> dated by my students. These are the rewards I
> experience here, but not the salary.

Most faculty members in both the education and information studies departments consider working with students and
conducting their own research as chief rewards of the job. A veteran faculty member described his role as a professor:

> The concept of teaching is at the core of what we
> do here, even though we're called something
> other than teacher. I think teaching and then the
> creation and dissemination of new knowledge
> would be just about right... Teaching gives me
> the greatest satisfaction. I feel really energized
> when I come from the classroom, particularly
> when I feel that I did a good job. I really do come
> alive in front of the classroom because I can share
> my work with them and the work of others. It's
> just fun for me.

An education faculty member with a reputation for working
closely with his students commented on his greatest pleasures
and satisfaction from the job:

> Far and away, it's working with students. That's
> why I do this work. My greatest satisfaction comes
> from when I'm in a classroom or working with an
> individual student and it feels like we're going
> somewhere—when something's happening.

An assistant professor in information studies acknowledged that he was surprised at how much he liked working
with students:

> I actually think I always knew that I would like
> working with students. But I guess I find it
> rewarding to an extent that I didn't necessarily
> anticipate.

Not counting Fridays, Saturdays, or Sundays, GSE&IS professors report working a little more than 11 hours each day. It is likely that most faculty members work an equal amount of time on Friday, and most report working at least eight hours over the typical weekend. Taken together, faculty members probably work an average of about 65 hours each week. One assistant professor described his intense worklife by saying, "I'm usually here (Moore Hall) six days a week. It used to be seven, but now I stay home on Saturdays. I read the newspaper, and then I work until about 6:00 or 7:00 at night. Sunday afternoon I come here and print things out, send faxes, and prepare for Monday's class." Somewhat more than a third of faculty members' time (38%) is spent on research, slightly more than a third (34%) on teaching and mentoring students, and the other third is allocated among university and community service, professional development, and other activities. About half of their work time is spent at UCLA (52%), while about a quarter of it is spent at home and the other quarter "elsewhere." Had we measured where time was spent on Fridays through Sundays the percentage spent at home and elsewhere would have been substantially higher.

Research

A Typical Research Day

Faculty members try to clear away entire blocks of time (full days when possible) for research. These research days are set aside for fieldwork, or for analyzing and writing articles and books that emerge from their research. Faculty members need dedicated time for analyzing data and writing because concentration is required. An education professor who also serves as an administrator explained:

> I never tried to write much here. There's a hustle and a bustle, even on quiet days, around the hallway. If you try to write in your office, shut the door, there's always somebody asking you for

something, go have coffee. Even if they didn't do
that, and you just thought they were going to do
that, you never—I just can't concentrate that way.

It is common for GSE&IS faculty to spend their research
days off campus. Many professors have home offices where
they report being more productive than they are at their campus offices. One professor commented:

I write in my home office. I've done it for years. I
live in an area that is very quiet and I look at the
mountains and I get inspired. It's not that I do not
like the university. It's simply that the university
has too many distractions to do good writing.

Another faculty member explained why he leaves the campus to write:

If no one knows where I am, they can't get at me.
If I'm out at my house, they have to drive all the
way out there to bug me. I turn the phones off. I
have switches on all of them. The [answering]
machine is on but I can't hear it. I feel safe. I can
write and think.

Because few classes are offered on Fridays, some faculty
members designate Fridays as writing days. Breaks between
academic quarters and summers also are often devoted exclu-
sively to research and writing. As one professor explained:

The place just feels a little more peaceful, and I'm
sure I tend to be a little more reflective, and perhaps do a little more writing during those times
than during the regular quarter when everything's bustling. Summers are definitely different.

An information studies professor commented about divid-
ing time between teaching and writing:

Then I have writing days. I love them! There
aren't enough of them! I do best when I have a

whole day to write. I've been writing recently in little bits and pieces, but if I have a whole day, I can get a whole lot more done. Six hours for me all at once is much more productive than six hours spread out over a couple of weeks. So, if possible, I have writing days. I used to have them once a week, but this quarter I'm finding that almost impossible.

The Research Process

Defining a typical day is somewhat artificial as most professors describe the boundaries between campus and home as fluid or blurred. One education professor described her worklife in the following way:

> You know the thing about our work is we are never separated from it. I mean, my study is next to my bedroom, so I'll wander in there at all times of the day and night. You know, there it is! It didn't go away! And you carry it with you. In your laptop; you carry it with you in your thoughts.

Most professors think of research as an individual activity not as a systematic process. Not surprisingly, the range of research conducted in the school is highly varied, ranging from critical analysis, evaluation, historical and experimental studies, to ethnographic and survey research. But, different from the Anderson School where much of the research is based on secondary data, most research conducted in the GSE&IS is based on data collected from the field.

Qualitative research projects (especially ethnographic studies) are complex, and drawing lines between data-gathering and analysis is not as straightforward as it is with quantitative research projects. Also, developing durable and trusting relationships with subjects is of crucial importance with qualitative studies, requiring substantial investments of time. On the other hand, faculty members who conduct survey research spend a great deal more time designing the studies, selecting samples, and developing instruments than do qualitative researchers. They also must pay close attention to sources of bias and have a good knowledge of statistical procedures. Most large studies are supported with extramural funds and require principal investigators to seek and secure funding, work within the university's and the funding agencies' rules and regulations, prepare budgets, manage funds, write reports and often organize conferences. Professors who work on their own or who do their work in libraries—historians and philosophers—have few such requirements. Nevertheless, even with these large variations in mind, research projects tend to follow six steps.

Generate ideas. First, an idea must be generated. Often, ideas for new studies are triggered by social and political events that intersect with professors' interests. For instance during the course of this study, faculty members launched new research projects to improve public school management, develop new curricula, help teacher union officials collaborate with administrators, and provide state-of-the-art information systems to libraries, to name but a few. One professor said the passage of two state-wide propositions that curtailed services to undocumented immigrants and ended affirmative action caused her and a colleague to launch a study of their impact. The 1991 police beating of Rodney King and the subsequent Los Angeles riots prompted another faculty member in 1994 to establish a research project with colleagues at the University of Southern California to document organizational changes in the Los Angeles Police Department. Research projects also emerge from casual conversations with colleagues, or from the interests of students. One information studies professor described a casual conversation in which she and a colleague from education "were talking about things and kicking around some ideas. We said, 'well wouldn't it be really cool if we...'" After some more discussion they had designed a study that the National Science Foundation decided to support.

Other professors develop their research in traditional ways, such as visiting the library to read, leading to development of new ideas or lines of inquiry. One professor said that after he gets an idea, he goes to the library to dig more deeply as part of the conceptualization stage:

> It includes going to the library and doing the research—looking at what other people are doing in this area. The whole idea of not wanting to reinvent the wheel is really important.

Find financial support. Second, financial support must be found. A substantial number of faculty members regularly seek and obtain research grants that exceed $100,000. Extramural sources include government agencies, the US departments of Education and Labor, the National Science Foundation, state agencies, and private foundations—the Spencer, Carnegie, Alfred P. Sloan, Kellogg Foundations, The Pew Charitable Trusts, and others. Sometimes faculty members reply to requests for proposals or submit pre-proposals, while in other cases research grants grow out of conversations between foundation officials and faculty members.

Most faculty members bypass UCLA's development office—which is supposed to help attract research money—in favor of developing their own personal relationships with government or foundation officials. Wishing to avoid unnecessary red tape and delays, many professors also make end-runs around UCLA's Office of Contract and Grant Administration at initial stages of the process. In 1997 the school hired a chief financial officer and a business office specialist who have helped to streamline the proposal preparation process. One professor said she thought the process had improved at the school level, but she remained critical, as did other faculty members, of the campus office of contracts and grants. She said:

> I'm not a 'last minute' person. I'm actually a 'prepare in advance' person [but] people don't answer their emails. They don't answer their telephones. They don't help. And then once you get a grant, managing the money is virtually impossible.

Some faculty members prefer to support their research by cobbling together existing resources, often taking advantage of small academic senate grants. Others seek no funding (especially philosophers, political scientists, and historians), saying they prefer working without support and being responsible to no one but themselves.

Begin the work. If faculty members succeed in securing necessary funding, they next prepare to begin the work. Because most research is done with human beings, its success ultimately depends on positive working relationships with external agencies where the research subjects are found. One professor described developing these relationships as difficult because they have to be "handled in a very sensitive way. You have to tell people who you are and why you're doing it and what their payoff will be. It just can't be about your payoff." Developing trust and convincing potential subjects of a mutual benefit can take a significant amount of time. One professor spoke of working in a school for two years before she asked the teachers to participate in her research project.

Research projects involving human subjects must be reviewed and cleared by the Human Subject Protection Committee. The university has established elaborate procedures that must be followed to protect subjects who could be at risk. But the reviews for approval can be daunting. Some faculty members regard the human subjects committee as a significant obstacle. One professor said:

> This committee was established to protect human subjects from risk in medical experiments. Extending it to the social sciences was a big mistake. They're terribly conservative and see risk everywhere. Once they get you in their clutches, you can be subject to inordinate delays and unnecessary demands that screw up your relationships you've worked so hard to establish in the field.

Conduct study. Next is the actual work of conducting a study. Defining when preparation ends and conducting the research begins differs according to the designs and methods of research projects. For some faculty members who do qualitative applied research, conducting the project includes building personal relationships with sponsors and subjects, developing strategies to feed back results, and collecting data. Qualitative researchers describe their work as messy because they spend hours in the field and regard everything in their environments as data, which they collect. One professor who works with a large research team of students, faculty members, and teachers from participating schools was struggling when we interviewed her to organize and maintain a database of hundreds of fieldnotes, summaries of videotapes, and records of emails exchanged among members of the research team.

Researchers who use quantitative or experimental methods, or who analyze secondary quantitative data, exist in a more orderly world. They typically spend less time in the field and more time working on campus in their offices or with campus research units.

Gather and prepare data. For either kind of research, graduate students are of critical importance. While some professors prefer to be engaged in the details of data gathering and preparing data for analysis, others delegate much of those responsibilities to graduate students. In those cases, professors serve as supervisors, meeting with the students at regular intervals to guide the process. One professor explained:

> I train and supervise them, but they do most of the work getting the files cleaned and ready to run. Then I do most of the inferential statistics though occasionally somebody will work with me on that part.

Working closely with graduate students in this way has benefits for both professors and students. Professors can depend on a ready pool of assistants, some of whom already have experience in conducting research. One faculty member described the school's "very rich layer of doctoral research assistants who bring knowledge and experience" to the research. For their part, students gain valuable experience working as apprentices, side-by-side with their mentors.

Publish results. Finally, results are written up and published. Many faculty members describe writing and publishing as both rewarding and frustrating. Frustrations are usually a reflection of a lack of time. Rewards come when professors see the tangible product of their hard work. But completing a manuscript and waiting for it to be published can take years. Journal articles make take from six months to two years or more to be published, while books can take even longer. One faculty member who had worked for five years with a team of students took a sabbatical leave coupled with a summer and wrote a book on the results of his research. He said:

> It was like having a gun to my head. It was terribly hard to stay focused, to screen out diversions and plug away day after day. But I had a contract from a good publisher and six months to finish. It was a time of discipline for me.

Not all faculty members wait until the end of their research projects to publish. Some write as they go, publishing articles as findings emerge. Graduate students often are important at this stage as well, both as resources and as collaborators. The norm is to share authorship with graduate students when they make substantive contributions.

Teaching

A Typical Teaching Day

Now we turn to the faculty's perception of typical teaching days. As we discussed earlier, faculty members have difficulty clearly separating their activities into discrete categories because teaching, mentoring students, conducting research, and providing service (working on university committees, community work, etc.) often run together. Nevertheless, most professors try to set aside distinct days for teaching as they do with research. Student mentoring and service are harder to classify because they blend with both. Despite these complexities, what follows could be called a typical teaching day.

For many faculty members, teaching usually is limited to the two or three days a week they are on campus (the other days are reserved for off-campus writing and fieldwork). In addition to being available in the classroom and to meet with students, professors on these days attend to department and university committee meetings and administrative duties. As one education professor put it, "When I come to Moore Hall, I pretty much come to meet and to teach."

Most professors say they usually spend from two to four hours preparing for each hour of class. Classes usually meet one day a week for four hours, so about half of a professor's day is taken up being in class with students. Many professors say they begin their teaching days at home, thinking how they are going to use the four-hour block of time and how they want the class to flow. On campus they gather notes and discussion guides, overheads, videotapes, or other teaching aids before stepping into the classroom.

One unusually conscientious education professor spoke about his pattern and the reasons for it as he prepared for class:

> I've taught this course now maybe seven years. I still put in about three hours to every hour of preparation. So, if I teach a four-hour class, I usually put in about 12 hours of preparation. And that doesn't include reading students' work. That's separate. When I first started teaching I really felt the importance of being prepared, knowing what was happening in the literature. So when I walk into a class I'd like to think that I have a pretty firm grasp of what other people are doing related to this topic. And I know what I'm doing. I want my students to be right up to date with the latest in the field. And that takes a lot of time.

Teaching days usually include office hours scheduled directly before or after class. This may be the only time a professor is available for consultation without a special appointment.

The university's tradition of shared governance produces a continuous schedule of meetings for consultation—committees of the campus academic senate, school-wide meetings, department and division meetings, committees on student admissions, fellowships, academic personnel, and others. Faculty members try to arrange on-campus teaching days to coincide with these meetings. Teaching days also include spontaneous meetings just because colleagues happen to be on campus that day. A faculty member observed:

> There are days that are sort of non-stop meetings. My calendar's pretty full. If it were the case every day, I wouldn't like it at all, but I don't mind those days because I sort of run on automatic pilot … interacting with people, getting engaged in interesting conversations.

Some faculty members complain that too much time is taken up in meetings even while acknowledging that meetings help create social cohesion. One professor said:

> There's not enough time in the day, and the demands of governance and participation in the department stuff don't bring me a particular amount of pleasure. To tell you the truth, the amount of stuff related to committees or personnel things or department stuff really takes up a huge amount of time. And there are times when I walk into a classroom less prepared than I'd like to be.

Another professor complained, "We have endless meetings. We don't make decisions, and we revisit the same issues over and over, year after year."

Amidst a professor's heavy schedule of meetings, colleagues, students, and administrators often bump into them unexpectedly, or notice an open door and ask for some time. Even if professors close their doors to avoid interruptions, teaching days with their preparation time, class time, office hours, administrative work, meetings, and socializing often run at a frenzied pace.

The Teaching Process

The teaching process can differ from professor to professor, depending on whether he or she is teaching a core course or elective, and on whether a class is new or has been taught for years. But in general, the teaching process can be divided into the following four steps.

Initiate course. First, a new course has to be initiated by a faculty member—or at the division or program level. Faculty members who belong to a particular program or division come together periodically, or perhaps annually, to review the curriculum and decide what will be offered in the coming year. One education professor explained:

> It's largely a division discussion where we look at the lineup of names and faculty who are going to be around and not on sabbatical, or bought out by projects... It's a division discussion, but there's some leeway, so I have a say in the kinds of things that I teach, and it's a fairly voluntary system, where you see a need and respond and do it.

The significantly smaller information studies faculty works on curriculum at the department level

Sometimes existing courses (particularly core courses) are modified to improve them or bring them up to date. New courses are usually the inspiration of one or more faculty members who come up with a new idea. Core courses typically require more faculty consultation and review than electives, and new courses that are developed as parts of whole new programs require extensive review.

Generally, faculty members have wide discretion in what they teach. One observed:

> This autonomy is terribly important. It enables
> me to connect my students with the changing
> field in a creative way. And it's fun to sometimes
> teach a course about something you love, just for
> the fun of it!

Some academic programs like the Educational Leadership
Program and Teacher Education Program are less flexible than
others because of time constraints or because they must fulfill
state requirements. The faculty director of the 40-month-long
Educational Leadership Program explained, "We must fit 100
hours of instruction into a very tight schedule each quarter so
every course must compete for time." In these cases, the initia-
tion of new courses is naturally more constrained.

Prepare course materials. Next, course material must be
prepared. Professors put a lot of time into thinking through the
content and overall structure of the courses they teach, ensuring
they are up to date with the latest research in the field. But
because most classes are seminars, GSE&IS professors do not
prepare elaborate lectures as do their colleagues in the
Anderson School and some other departments. Often they leave
planning exact activities until the day of class.

Faculty members in both education and information studies
say they rarely use textbooks, a reflection of the changing
nature of both fields, as well as faculty autonomy, and the fact
that most courses are seminars of 15 or fewer students. One faculty member commented, "There just isn't a textbook that does
what I want to do… If I published a text then that's what I'd
have to use for the next six to eight years, and I don't want to
do that." But assembling readings is a labor-intensive process,
especially for new courses. Because of the limited administrative help that is available, faculty members frequently assemble
their own readers and take them to local copy shops for repro-
duction. They also are responsible for ordering their own books
and reserving audio-visual equipment from the school's
Educational Technology Unit.

Teach. Next comes the actual teaching. Small classes require
student participation. One professor explained, "We don't think

of any of our courses as a large lecture forum. It's heavily inter-active, heavily workshop based." Many faculty members encourage students to learn to work in teams. "It's going to be required after they graduate," one professor said, "so we get them used to it through projects. Students like the team tasks although they think it's a lot of work."

Autonomy allows faculty members to experiment with dif-ferent ways of teaching. One said:

> Many times experiments fail. I mean what's an experiment for, right? It's to try something out. If it doesn't work, you drop it and you go on. And so in many ways I have to say I've failed. But I look at it like Michael Jordan who says, "I've shot 3,000 shots that never went in." Well I've tried things that just bombed! No question about it.

Grade students. Finally, students are graded. Professors rarely grade student performance with objective tests. One young professor said, "Grading's a load of BS. It's so subjec-tive. I kind of go, 'hmmm, feels like a B to me.' And I'm told I'm the hardest grader here!" Most faculty members say they are mainly concerned that students understand concepts and so they evaluate them on attendance, participation in class, and on written term papers. One professor described the rhythm of the academic quarter as frenzied at first "but when the quarter ends, I wind up sitting here in the office or at home by the fireplace with a stack of papers that I have to read."

Most graduate students are given As, and some are given Bs. Only in extreme cases are they given Cs, a grade that is tantamount to failing. To the extent that low-performing stu-dents are systematically weeded out, negative evaluations are usually rendered by the faculty as a group (in programs or divisions) on the basis of first-year screening examinations, comprehensive written examinations, and preliminary oral examinations.

Feedback on the Processes

Feedback on Teaching

Faculty members are required to have students evaluate their courses using one of two standard evaluation forms. Results of evaluations are supposed to help professors improve their teaching, and they are also used in promotions. There is a general lack of enthusiasm about these evaluations among most faculty members for a variety of reasons. Results often are returned to professors weeks and sometimes months after courses have ended, making it difficult to incorporate the feedback into future classes. Many professors complain that standard evaluations do not capture what is most important:

> [My] course got good evaluations so that helps.
> But did I succeed in helping people become more
> thoughtful? How do you really measure that? I'm
> not so sure I know the answer.

Another faculty member said that she thought success was best measured by whether her students got turned on and stayed with the field, but that standardized evaluation forms did not measure it.

Most professors, especially the more experienced ones, said they learn to watch for informal student feedback and make adjustments. Some say they pay close attention to whether or not students are keeping up with the reading and if the quality of class discussion is high. Most said they knew when they weren't reaching their students. One professor said:

> It's like the air goes out of the class. There's no
> spirit, no 'ah ha's'. It feels dead. And soon I feel
> dead. Then you know you've got a problem.

Another form of feedback comes from the students after they have finished a course. Most faculty members say they are content if their students demonstrate they understood the subject matter or if they say they can think more creatively. One professor gave an example:

> What's really important to me, fundamentally, is helping people develop… a kind of rigorous as well as reflective cast of mind and to come at research, to come at inquiry with a curiosity, with a willingness to see things a little differently, with a thoughtfulness, with a care, and a carefulness.

Another important source of feedback is whether or not courses continue to be offered. When colleagues or students urge a faculty member to offer a course, it is usually considered an important indicator of success.

Although the office of student services conducts surveys infrequently—the last one was conducted in 1993—to gauge student satisfaction, and some programs poll their students from time to time, there are no systematic feedback loops to incorporate student preferences.

Feedback on Research

Professors were unanimous in their agreement that research should influence policy or practice or both. Many reflect an altruistic desire, saying they want to "give something back to society." A Latina professor explained:

> People of color… have to do stuff that impacts people in our multiple communities… My research has to be action oriented, it has to have a consequence, it has to have an end that I can see which makes a difference. I get frustrated sometimes that it has such a small impact and I'd love it to make more of a difference. But I think my work is about trying to make a difference in my multiple communities.

Research products range from refereed journal articles, books, conference presentations and papers, to speeches, editorials, and commentaries written for general audiences. The Graduate School of Education and Information Studies is the top-ranked public institution among its peers in the country in part because the faculty is so productive.

In addition, faculty members provide expert testimony for governmental bodies—including Congress and state legislatures—on policy issues including standardized testing, student financial aid, student access to education, and uses of information and technology. Many also serve as consultants for governmental bodies at the state and federal levels as well as for school districts and colleges and universities. The school's public information officer plays an important dissemination role by injecting research findings into public debate through the news media and school publications. Some recent studies that have found their way into the popular press carried headlines like:

> "Keeping up with Technology is a Major Source of Stress for the Nation's College Faculty, UCLA Study Shows"

> "SUNY and UCLA Researchers Lead Study Seeking Solutions to Electronic-Record Preservation Crisis"

> "UCLA Professor Finds the Adult-Child Relationships in Early Child Care are Key to Future School Success"

> "Academic and Political Engagement Among Nation's College Freshmen is at All-time Low, UCLA Study Finds"

> "UCLA Study Finds Charter Schools Not Yet Living up to Promises"

> "LAPD Morale Down Since 1990s"

Feedback on the impact of faculty members' research is harder to discern. We asked faculty members to identify the beneficiaries of their work. One education professor who does research in the public schools replied:

> I think the teachers are benefiting because they're really having an opportunity to engage with their

> colleagues... I think that the principal is benefit-
> ing because she's got a whole school full of teach-
> ers who are involved in inquiry. I think the kids
> at the school are benefiting because they are
> involved in inquiry. I think that my graduate stu-
> dents are benefiting because they're also in the
> process of learning... I think that the math edu-
> cation community will benefit because we're
> learning some things that I think, in the long run,
> will end up being really important to them.

Sometimes clear cause-and-effect relationships can be
drawn between professors' research and changes in practice. A
faculty member who had studied industrial work systems testi-
fied before a California senate committee on his findings. The
committee was considering how to provide public training
funds to companies to improve their productivity and human
resource practices. The professor's testimony led the committee
to write new legislation to target training monies to companies
trying to implement high performance work systems.

But for the most part there is no tracking of a research project's impact on society. Professors trust that if their work is
published it ultimately will be read, and through this channel it
may influence policy or practice. A professor who was studying
education in China in the late 1960s and early 1970s offered an
interesting example of how this assumption works. He
described how he became passionate about his research,
learned Chinese, and gained access to the country's educational elite at a time when most scholars believed it would be
impossible. He spent a number of years doing research in vil-
lage schools and published the results in books and articles. At
the time, he said, "The Chinese were not looking at themselves.
They were bemused with my work and they didn't really take
it seriously." But on a recent trip to China, he spoke with some
second generation Chinese education scholars. He said:

> It turns out these younger researchers had been
> quietly reading my stuff. And there was very lit-

tle else for them to read because so little had been written, given the access and language barriers. Once China began to modernize, education became a high priority. So the Chinese published my book that had been published originally in English without permission—I guess imitation is the greatest form of flattery!

A final outcome of faculty members' research is the next generation of educational scholars and policy leaders. Most faculty members take great pleasure in mentoring students, especially as they work on their dissertations and begin to develop as professional researchers. Preparing a dissertation is a grueling process for most doctoral students, and the quality of the mentoring provided by professors who chair their dissertations can spell the difference between success and failure. Yet, there is no formal feedback loop to help professors learn about their impact on students. They depend instead on informal feedback (communications with students after they graduate) to evaluate their success as mentors. In the course of our investigation we were surprised to find that the Graduate Division, which oversees graduate education at UCLA, surveys doctoral graduates each year on their graduate school experience. Included is an evaluation of their dissertation committee chair's mentoring. According to an administrator, the information is sent back to the school but is not provided to professors, nor is it used in personnel actions.

Now having examined the school's culture, work patterns, and core processes, we turn to an analysis of GSE&IS as a dynamic organization. We begin with a discussion of key forces impinging on the school, how the school responds to them, and the consequences of the action.

Forces for Change

Our research left little doubt that two external forces have had a powerful impact on the GSE&IS: Like the Anderson School, the GSE&IS is struggling to adjust to a continuing decline in the proportion of funding coming from state revenues. But it faces another driving force not encountered by Anderson: The emergence of both education and information technology as high-profile, national issues.

Declining State Funding

Until 1991, faculty in the Graduate School of Education and Information Studies had access to a wide range of resources. Research travel grants, sabbatical leaves, administrative support, copying, Federal Express services, telephones, faxes, and computers were available and taken for granted. The annual budget process was of little interest to most professors and few of them really knew—or cared—how resources were actually distributed. Cost overruns on research grants were commonplace. Only after some invisible spending limit was crossed were eyebrows ever raised.

State funds allocated to the University of California system have been declining for the last 30 years. In 1966, somewhat less than half of all university resources were state funds, but by 1998 the total was less than 20%. In 1991, reductions in state spending forced by a major economic recession required deep and permanent cuts in UCLA's budget. In just five years, from 1992 to 1997, the proportion of state funding for the school declined from 57% to 48% of the total ($18 million).

The effect of dwindling public resources has produced an increased awareness among the faculty and administration of the need to live within constrained budgets. And a growing number of faculty members have begun to acknowledge the need to seek out new private sources of revenue. For instance, one assistant professor said:

> I'm getting the feeling that it's going to be harder to get release time from classes. The chair has intimated that… It's just like the money's not there for lecturers and so on. So it's sounding like more people are going to be teaching full loads and it's going to be tougher to get release time.

He continued, "I think next year I'll have to start looking around for more money."

The Rise of Education and Information Technology as National Issues

The emergence of education and information technology as high profile national issues in the mid-1990s provided new and unanticipated opportunities for GSE&IS. As we mentioned earlier, in 1992 an entrepreneurial administrator was hired as dean to help the school adapt to a changing environment. The dean explained that he took the job fully aware that the faculty would have to learn to live within constrained resources and that new sources of revenue would have to be found:

> It was clear from the early 1990s, following the decline of California's economy, that we would have to come together as a faculty to understand the cost constraints. At the same time we would have to think about our programs—the ones that existed as well as new ones—as revenue producers.

We found persuasive evidence that the decline in state funds produced a dramatic change in the school's stream of revenue. In 1986, 63% of the school's revenue came from general (state) funds. By 1997, that figure had declined by more than 40%. At the same time, revenue generated from sales and service had increased from 11% in 1986 to 30% in 1997. Similarly, funds from private sources had increased during the same period from 4% to 12%.

Other Forces for Change

In 1994 two significant local events began to forge a new consciousness among the faculties of the Graduate School of Education and the Graduate School of Library and Information Science – a merger creating a single, two-department school, and the introduction of Responsibility Center Management (RCM). Both events signaled to faculty leadership that California's economic slowdown had already constrained resources, and that would surely affect day-to-day life as it had been known.

The merger. To help meet the budget shortfall, the UCLA chancellor implemented a series of phased budget reductions between 1991 and 1993 to reduce staff, create early retirement incentives for faculty, and cut some academic programs. But another multi-million dollar budget shortfall in 1994 caused the chancellor to develop a plan to eliminate or reconfigure five of UCLA's professional schools—Architecture and Urban Planning, Nursing, Public Health, Social Welfare, and Library and Information Science. The Graduate School of Library and Information Science (GSLIS) was targeted to be disbanded, and its faculty members were to be distributed to other academic units—probably most would have come to the Graduate School of Education.

The shock of the rapid decision to abolish and reconfigure the five professional schools—many faculty members felt it was made without sufficient consultation—activated long-standing tensions between the faculty and the administration. These tensions dated back to the loyalty oath controversy of the early 1950s when University of California professors were forced to deny any Communist party affiliation. Faculty leaders had charged the administration with abandoning fundamental academic values for the sake of political expediency (Stewart, 1971). The restructuring in 1994 deepened faculty suspicions and activated feelings of mistrust.

The dean of the Graduate School of Education suggested, and the faculty agreed, as a professional kindness and a strategic opportunity, to invite the GSLIS faculty to become a department in the Graduate School of Education. The merger also meant that the Graduate School of Education would become a department. Despite some education faculty grumbling, the new two-unit school was renamed the Graduate School of Education and Information Studies.

The restructuring reactivated the lingering mistrust between the faculty and administration. One senior IS faculty member described her feelings about the merger:

It's created a culture that's gone from seeing ourselves as winners and on top of the heap, or being
part of a wonderful school, to feeling kind of
sorry for ourselves. I just loathe that. I've always
felt that I worked in a world-class institution. I've
never felt like a loser, and I don't like being surrounded by that kind of feeling. You can get
sucked into that victim mentality. I just hate it.

Another IS faculty leader described the first years as angry,
and like a shotgun marriage. She continued:

It's building a whole new internal culture and a
whole new set of relationships... and a different
relationship with the field... There are very few
schools in this field that are not autonomous...
and they tend to be at lesser universities. [That] is
one of the reasons we fought so hard for a creation
of a new school with a merged name. The original
proposal was to make us a department in education. Most of us said, 'If that happens, my vita's
out of here so fast!'... So that's always been a
point of contention and whenever anyone brings
up the phrase, "Graduate School of Education" as
an opening... there is no such thing!

While some education department faculty members enthusiastically welcomed the merger and the new opportunities it represented, others did not. Some disparaged IS as a warrantable
field of study while others worried that the new department
would draw off scarce resources and worsen education's budget problems. Attempts were made to co-locate faculty members
in one or both buildings that had housed the separate schools,
but neither department wanted to move. The much larger education faculty was accustomed to Moore Hall while the IS faculty was dispirited by the reorganization and none wanted to
move to Moore Hall. Making the merger even more difficult was
the administrative and academic apparatus that accompanies

departmental status. A separate administrative structure, faculty review process, academic oversight, plus separate meetings and housing ensured that integration of the two departments occurred slowly. One IS faculty member observed:

> Being a department instead of a school adds another layer of bureaucracy, which adds to the time that we put in. I don't think the time spent at departmental committees has increased all that much... but we also have school committees... But then you don't have a voice and I don't think that's nearly so much of a pressure on the education people.

An academic administrator observed that tension between the two faculties was inherent in the disproportionate sharing of power:

> Both departments are adversaries. Deans typically come from education... and they have the control and the power. The fiction was that it's a merger. Really, IS lost its school status.

Data from our study revealed only limited interaction between the two departments. However, there are indications that initial anxiety between the two departments may be subsiding. One IS faculty member says that she likes the education department's emphasis on doctoral studies and research and its positive impact on IS:

> I think my department's embraced technology better, but if we could only get the education thing figured out at the school level there's so much potential. [It] would be an unabashedly good thing. It would help our department. It would help us achieve some of our goals, fulfill our mission a little bit better.

A senior IS faculty member said that now with much of the conflict behind them, many of her colleagues are looking to a cooperative future between the two departments. She said:

> Let's look to the future and... build on our
> strengths and build something new... This is our
> third full year and we're getting to the point of
> thinking of ourselves as a unified school and
> thinking in terms of those strengths and what can
> be done in multimedia and information technol-
> ogy, and information technology and learning

Another IS faculty member said she thought the hiring of
some new IS faculty members would also hasten a better integration of the two departments:

> We need to think of this as pre-merger and, post-
> merge, I'll bet the relationships across the depart-
> ments come as a result of our new faculty who
> see it as an attractive place to be because they
> wanted to cross departmental lines.

Responsibility Center Management

Despite UCLA's internal restructuring, there was little doubt
that growth in public revenues had subsided. The chancellor
began to restructure the internal workings of the university so
that it could respond more quickly to changes, including fiscal
realities. He acknowledged:

> The resource flows within the university are
> obscured, and our ability to make fully informed
> resource allocations is weakened accordingly. We
> lack well-defined incentives for academic entre-
> preneurship [or resources development] and for
> banking resources for planned future investment.
> Our financial information system does not ade-
> quately support dynamic financial management,
> or make accountability for fiscal performance clear.

In 1994, the chancellor and his top staff decided to begin the
restructuring by pushing decisions about costs and revenues
down to individual academic and administrative units where

deans would now have sufficient information and authority to make choices. They believed that by giving individual units fiscal control, internal markets would be created to allocate increasingly scarce resources. UCLA drew heavily on models of Responsibility Center Management (RCM) that were being tried at Indiana University, the University of Southern California, the University of Michigan, the University of Pennsylvania and others. Three academic units—the Graduate School of Education & Information Studies, The Anderson School, and the Division of Physical Sciences at the College of Letters and Science—were chosen as simulation sites to test how RCM would actually work in practice.

Faculty members at GSE&IS reacted with suspicion and hostility toward the business principles they were being asked to embrace. To many, the new language of customers, products, outputs, and markets was offensive. An education professor complained, "Talking about students as customers is obnoxious. I mean they aren't customers. They're students. That kind of language just doesn't belong in an educational institution." It soon became clear that many faculty members were contemptuous of business and held corporate values in low regard. One professor said, "This is not a business. I'm simply not enthusiastic about participating in boardroom culture." Other faculty members were concerned that harsh business practices would surely follow RCM, possibly threatening their autonomy. A survey of GSE&IS revealed that more than a quarter of the faculty felt that RCM would lead to staff layoffs. One professor described his fears:

> In the future we may become just like business
> with a greater reliance on part-time workers and
> job sharing. I see a much less comfortable world
> than the one we've been used to.

RCM was tested in the simulation units for two years. Its introduction barely caused a ripple in The Anderson School which, as a reflection of the business world, already practiced many RCM principles. But in GSE&IS its merits were hotly debated. While RCM failed to penetrate the school's academic core, the struggle served to raise faculty members' consciousness: Growing revenue could no longer be taken for granted, and it would be necessary to constrain spending and find fresh sources of private revenue.

The School Responds

Internal Efficiencies

Nowhere could the effect of reduced resources be seen more clearly than in the education department chair's efforts to produce new efficiencies (and quality improvements) by better matching the supply and demand of courses. For historical reasons, the Department of Education had always been course-heavy. Doctoral students are required to take a minimum of 18 four-unit courses before sitting for written comprehensive examinations. Not surprisingly, a large number of courses were on the books though some were rarely offered. This accumulation of courses was partly the result of inattention, but it also served the purpose of obscuring the actual teaching process. Most faculty members exercised their autonomy by deciding which courses to teach and at what hours. One result was a proliferation of small seminars that enrolled only four or five students or courses that failed to enroll enough students to be taught at all. Another result was that students often complained of being unable to find courses they needed, when they needed them. At one department meeting in 1998, the chair surprised the faculty by beginning a conversation about aligning the supply of courses and student demand—a topic that had not been discussed in recent history. The chair recalled:

> It was clear that this could not work anymore. There were many new pressures on us to offer a more organized program. I didn't think we could afford the luxury of allowing faculty to teach these little courses only, and when they wanted to. So there was a fair amount of friendly pres-

sure exerted internally to try to offer a program
that provided a better balance between faculty
autonomy—allowing them to teach the things
they specialize in—and what the students needed
and wanted.

The program had been ranked for a decade or more as one
of the country's best education programs at a public university.
Beginning in 1992, the uncertainty caused by fiscal hardship
also created an opportunity to make deeper changes in the academic program. At least two people serving as department
chair during this period initiated conversations with the faculty
about strengthening student recruiting nationally. The expectation was that national recruiting would help the department
develop a national image and provide a richer student experience. There also had been discussions during this same period
of time, especially more recently when courses were being
pruned, to develop a less course-intensive program, emphasiz-
ing instead an apprenticeship model. A faculty member echoed
the sentiments of others when he said:

> There are people who have always taken mentor-
> ing seriously, and it's being talked about more.
> Spending a lot of time with students and teaching
> a full load and being involved in other efforts are
> spreading people pretty thin. It's something we
> really have to watch out for.

Finally, the chair began discussions with each of the five
departmental divisions about eliminating inactive students and
revamping their curricula. It was part of a larger effort to reduce
the overall size of the doctoral program. In fact, between 1992
and 1998, the doctoral program had been reduced 20%, from
349 to 281 students.

New Opportunities and Style of Leadership

At about the same time in the mid-1990s, education and information technology became national priorities—both center-

pieces of the president's domestic policy agenda. As a result, private foundations as well as federal agencies like the US Department of Education and the National Science Foundation increased the amount of funds available for research. For GSE&IS, this helped in some ways to compensate for the reduction in state revenue but not in the all-important general support category that was unaffected by these new monies.

Also in the mid-1990s, the school's development office was restructured to generate additional extramural funds. The development office formerly had consisted of a part-time person who was responsible for publications and keeping track of donors and significant alumni. The dean hired a new development officer who had substantial development experience at Harvard, the Claremont Colleges, and the University of Southern California. He reflects a new style of leadership demanded by an increasingly complex and competitive environment, and he conceptualizes the job differently than it had been in the past. The development director notes that GSE&IS has a young and anemic development program. He said, "Unlike Anderson, we don't have a bunch of people out there doing IPOs [Initial Public Offerings] every week." He continued:

> The flip side is that education is recognized to be a problem in our society. A big problem and a big priority, and so foundations, for example, are much easier for us to go after than they are for Anderson.

He says that while the merger was like a shotgun marriage and that much is still to be worked out between education and information studies, having two dynamic departments is a plus. He explained:

> But the problems [of the merger] aren't in the foreground. What's in the foreground is the opportunity that IS provides because it's a gem of a department. Absolutely! There are some wonderful people who are recognized nationally, and they're in the center of what is going on.

The director explains his role as a bridge rather than as a traditional fund-raiser. He explained how building new relationships between the school and external funding agencies was critical:

> If we know a faculty member is going to be in Chicago, we might say 'Would you go and stop in on such and such?' to help build the relationship... I think, you know, in an ideal world, what I do is just fun, because you're talking to people who care about the same issues that you care about, and you know, you're doing this over dinner or at lunch or you're sitting in their living room.

The director is clear about one thing: Even though most faculty leaders already are over-taxed, he needs their active support in order to do his job:

> I need to have faculty involved in what I'm doing and in particular, I need to have leadership at the school involved. Otherwise there's no way I can be successful. People aren't going to give money to me. They're going to give money to people who are doing the work at the school. My role is to just facilitate the relationship. I think faculty need to be more aware of what development is all about, what has been accomplished, and be willing to participate in what we do.

He makes it a point to keep in close touch with individual faculty members. One education professor explained how startling this new strategy was:

> I was sitting in my office one day and the damndest thing happened. [The development officer] had called for an appointment and when he came in and sat down he began asking me about my work. After I described my research he asked, 'How can we help you? Do you know about this

foundation or that one?' In my 20 years at UCLA, this had never happened. Development was always off in a dark corner and it had little effect on any of our lives.

Between 1992 and 1998, private gifts increased 224%, attesting to the wisdom of the new development strategy. In 1992, private gifts to education stood at only $369,000 but by 1998, they had increased to $1.2 million. Similarly, extramural funding grew by 38% during the same time, from $6 million in 1992 to $8.3 million in 1998.

Unexpected Consequences

But growth did not come without a cost. GSE&IS faculty members report spending somewhat more than a third of their time (37%) on research. More than a quarter of that time is spent acquiring resources. Put another way, professors report spending as much time writing proposals as they do writing and disseminating the results of their research for publication. An information studies professor said:

> It seems like I spend so much time scrambling to get money that I don't have time to do the research when I finally get it. It's almost like being an independent contractor, trying to get the resources to do research. A couple of times I've been able to get a buy-out from classes, and that certainly helps with time. But then you have to remember that teaching was the most rewarding part of my job.

For years GSE&IS faculty members complained about the lack of research infrastructure to support their grant-getting activities. The school's associate dean observed that the university's rules and regulations governing research had grown more stringent. But there had been no corresponding effort to provide faculty members with the assistance they needed to meet them. She said:

> The university has tightened up on faculty mem-
> bers' flexibility with their consulting—the num-
> ber of days you are allowed, at least on paper. It
> used to be sort of an open economy. Same thing
> with creating new companies. In the past, faculty
> members who started up new companies took all
> the profits, but now they've set up this third, third,
> third business about how profits are to be split.

Recognizing the difficult circumstances the faculty faced,
and the disincentives created by the university's increasingly
complex rules and regulations, in 1997 the associate dean hired
two respected financial managers from the central administration to help. "It's the best thing I've done this year," she said,
"because these are real money people and real problem
solvers." Nevertheless, many faculty members still feel that
they have to work against their own university to generate
extramural resources. One professor said:

> I think that UCLA unintentionally puts up obsta-
> cles. Getting a proposal out of the university is an
> ordeal. With [the new grant administrators] I
> think it's gotten a little smoother, but it used to be
> hell to get it out of the department. Nobody knew
> how to help. Then working with the [central
> administration's] office of contracts and grants...
> people don't answer their emails. They don't
> answer their telephones.

Nevertheless, faculty efforts paid off with the number of
grant awards rising from 48 in 1991-1992 to 171 in 1997-1998.
The value of the grant awards rose as well during the same time
period, from $7 million to $11.5 million.

New Programs and Rewards

A variety of new programs had sprung up since the early 1990s
partly in response to new opportunities and partly as a means
to produce private sources of revenue. One example is Center X,

so called because of its focus on the intersection of educational theory and practice. Center X houses a variety of research projects that aim to improve K-12 education: It organizes outreach activities aimed at local public schools, especially those in low-income neighborhoods; it offers a host of professional development courses for educators; and it runs the GSE&IS' Teacher Education Program. An education professor who heads Center X explained its role in the school as "developing teachers with passion, commitment, and resiliency."

Also in the early 1990s, the dean and a small group of faculty members began planning an alternatively scheduled doctoral program for working education professionals. By scheduling the Educational Leadership Program during off-hours, the program could be sanctioned by the university to charge additional fees, producing a new source of revenue for the school. The program spans 40 months and enrolls about 25 doctoral students each year who go through their coursework as a cohort. The program's academic director observed, "Charging fees produces revenue for the school, but it has a greater value by keeping us on the inventive edge, looking for better ways of teaching and helping our students learn."

A third program getting underway during this period was the School Management Program (SMP), which started as the academic arm of the Los Angeles Unified School District's reform effort. Developed jointly with The Anderson School, SMP provides management training for principals and lead teachers in southern California and other parts of the country.

According to most faculty members, programs like these have produced value for the school, both internally and externally, in a number of ways. For instance, Center X has fostered new models of collaborative research between the university and public school agencies to improve school practice. Other faculty members began working with United Teachers Los Angeles (the Los Angeles teachers' union) to help evaluate union-led programs for teachers. A faculty member who teaches in the Educational Leadership Program observed how it connects GSE&IS more closely with local K-12 and other higher education institutions. Also, as a financially independent program, it offers a place to innovate and to try out new ideas. He added:

> We can drop the ideas that don't work and then diffuse the successes back into the traditional program. We're working to come up with action research projects—alternatives to the traditional dissertation—that can really help the schools improve.

In a similar way, the School Management Program, though it has no core faculty members, offers training that draws on both education and management. Principals who are engaged in public school reform efforts take a series of courses designed to make them more effective managers and instructional leaders. The dean observed, "If you look at the numbers, it is a smashing success. The program now runs an annual revenue stream of between $2.5 million and $3 million dollars. If you look at it that way, it is a roaring success."

The effect has been to build new relationships and strengthen existing ones between GSE&IS faculty members and professional educators in the public schools and neighboring colleges. A former superintendent of the Los Angeles Unified School District commented:

> We've had a longstanding relationship with the center for research on evaluation standards and student testing (at GSE&IS) where we worked through many of the issues around standards. When the state came down with its pronouncements, we'd already been there. We had already developed standards, so it helped us ward off state politics.

One senior education professor added:

> In the old days everybody was doing their own individual research and there was no way to assess the impact on the schools. Well, since the

money ran out people have been asking, 'What are the schools of education doing to solve these problems?' The result has been to help us provide assistance to local school districts in a way we could never have done years back.

Another consequence of a new revenue-producing teaching program (the doctoral Educational Leadership Program) has been to intensify faculty members' and students' interest in outcomes. The program is to be completed in 40 months, and courses are scheduled in the evenings and weekends to accommodate working adults. Such tight time budgeting has naturally led faculty planners to ask, "What are we trying to accomplish? What skills and abilities must students possess at the conclusion?" Students pay a premium fee (about $9,500 per year compared to $4,700 for traditional students). Paying higher fees leads these older students to expect more than do traditional students, an attitude that is not lost on the faculty. The academic director commented:

> For the most part these students are gentle in their criticisms and demands, but we take them very seriously. We pay close attention to course evaluations, and when faculty members get poor marks we try to find out why so we can improve.

Disconnects from the Core

But there is an underside to the growth of new programs that are not directly connected to the core faculty. Some of the teaching done in the Educational Leadership Program and most instruction done in the School Management Program is done by practitioners who are hired as adjunct visiting professors and lecturers who lack ladder faculty status. In fact, the ranks of non-ladder faculty in GSE&IS grew by 38% between 1992 and 1998 to a total of 51—nearly equal to the total number of ladder faculty. A leading rationale for hiring practitioners—former school superintendents, teacher union leaders, and college presidents—is to infuse their contemporary and practical view-points into the classroom. On the other hand, appointing non-ladder faculty members is an easy way to augment the teaching staff when there are few incentives to attract autonomous and self-directed ladder faculty members into these new ventures.

But marginalizing this group of faculty and the programs in which they teach has now become a reality. Our analysis of social networks reveals a void in connections between the adjunct faculty, instructors in the School Management Program, and the rest of GSE&IS. The dean observed:

> The core faculty has other things to do. The result is isolation for the non-ladder faculty. This is an example of what happens when you don't build the links firmly enough into the core that is nurturing in both directions. You can see the deep wound that has to be dealt with.

The issue surfaced during the 1997 annual faculty retreat when someone asked whether or not non-ladder faculty should be included in the school's strategic planning. Pros and cons were considered, and the general sentiment was for inclusion because of adjuncts' experience outside the university. Next, the conversation turned to adjuncts' rights and responsibilities in the academic community. One faculty member said, "With no academic rights or responsibilities, we're unwittingly creating a second class of academic citizenship." There was general agreement, but the discussion ended without resolution. Later, the dean commented:

> The assumption is that the world would be better off if there were more lines between the core faculty and these new programs. In my gut I think that's probably right. The benefit would have to be in both directions. But it's an assumption we haven't pushed very far. I mean how different can people be and still be faculty? Wouldn't it be wonderful if people who really have different skill sets

> could come in and be a part of us without neces-
> sarily having to be just the same as we are?

In 1996 the dean was asked to take on added duties of becoming vice chancellor for budget and planning, and for a time he tried to do both. It soon became apparent that the two jobs were impossible to do simultaneously, so an interim dean was appointed and served for a year. The changes in leadership created uncertainty, making it difficult for the school to come to grips with many of the problems that were emerging. Despite strong leadership exerted by both department chairs, the faculty was feeling dispirited by the lack of continuity at the dean's level.

Summary

Faculty

By most faculty and staff members' accounts, the Graduate School of Education and Information Studies is a convivial place. Both faculty and staff members frequently interact with each other about their work, and professional relationships often spill over into social life. Despite initial unhappiness about the merger of education and information studies, faculty members in both departments voice hopes for increased synergy between the two. Money is not a key motivator for most education or information studies professors who instead value making positive contributions to society and protecting their autonomy around teaching and research. According to most faculty members, mentoring students also brings immense satisfaction.

GSE&IS faculty members report working an average of a little more than 11 hours each day, and most say that the lines between their home and work lives are blurred. About half of faculty members' work time is spent on campus, a quarter at home, and a quarter in the field. Working hours are split rather evenly between teaching, research, and service to the university and community.

Interestingly, faculty members had to pause and think before describing activities that would qualify as core process-es. The finding that faculty members do not regard teaching or research as core processes is not surprising. Teaching is consid-ered by most professors to be an integral part of day-to-day life that is guided by a combination of tradition; professors' interests; emerging social, political, and economic issues; and students' needs. Research, on the other hand, is regarded as a highly indi-vidual activity in contrast to a core process. While we were unable to achieve the level of precision we had hoped for in mapping these processes, we could discern stages that roughly marked the beginning, middle, and end of each of these processes.

Impact from External Forces

Some significant external forces had a discernable impact on the school. Reductions in public resources (a pattern that had begun in the 1970s and had accelerated in the early 1990s) pro-duced a growing awareness on the campus that resources had become limited.

A university-wide effort in the mid-1990s called Responsibility Center Management (RCM) aimed to decentral-ize decision-making about costs and revenues. GSE&IS was one of three test sites. RCM improved the school's financial opera-tions by making financial transactions more transparent and budget reports more intelligible, but it failed to penetrate the academic core. Slowed by university-wide skepticism on the part of the faculty and by the retirement of a chancellor who had championed the idea, RCM all but disappeared. In its place, uni-versity administrators decided to embark on strategic planning in cooperation with the academic senate. But within GSE&IS the faculty remained largely disinterested and uninvolved.

Also in the early to mid-1990s other changes were taking place at GSE&IS. A new entrepreneurial dean helped craft a merger between the former Graduate School of Library and Information Science and Graduate School of Education. Fortuitously, while the new school was struggling with reduc-tions in public resources, both education and information technology became high profile national issues. The new opportunities brought with them support for new research and academic programs in both departments.

Reductions in public revenue also enabled the school's leaders to make some changes already on the drawing board. For instance, the PhD program was reduced in size, and a program of national student recruiting was instituted to improve student quality. The education department also began to try to align the supply of courses with student demand. The chair asked faculty members to reduce the number of very small seminars and increase offerings among courses students needed when they wanted to take them.

The development office, formerly a small, inconspicuous operation, took on a heightened importance in the new environment. Its new director became an important actor, offering assistance to faculty members, helping with strategic planning, visiting foundations, and generating substantial amounts of new monies. Grants and contracts for research programs also grew significantly during this time as individual faculty members wrote an unusually large number of proposals. Many complained about the lack of an effective infrastructure to help them with outside funding, but steps were taken to streamline the proposal writing process including creating accurate budget estimates.

A variety of new programs—including Center X, the undergraduate education minor, the School Management Program, and the Educational Leadership Program—also were created during this period either in response to new opportunities, to produce new revenues, or both. These new programs were designed to connect the school more firmly with the professional education community, offering action research, teacher training, consulting assistance, and a doctoral program for working adults.

Changes

While these responses to the changing environment were for the large part positive, helping the school advance its research agenda and forge tighter relationships with the professional community, some negative consequences were also evident. Perhaps most significant was the increase in pressures on faculty members' time. During this period, professors developed an unprecedented number of new funding proposals for research. They also were asked to teach in these new programs while meeting existing teaching commitments. As a consequence, large numbers of non-ladder faculty members were hired to augment the regular faculty. The adjunct faculty, who also took on much of the student mentoring, taught an increasing number of courses. While these changes came about relatively quickly, most of the faculty and administrative staff remained unaware of the impact. Findings from the research reveal that despite these adjunct faculty members' contributions, they live on the margins of academic life with limited faculty rights, seldom interacting with the regular faculty.

Finally, turnover of deans made it difficult for the school to maintain a consistent focus because of the uncertainty caused by the lack of stability in the top leadership.

Addendum: From Late 1998 to 2001

At the end of 1998 it became apparent that the GSE&IS had, unknown to the faculty, accrued a million dollar deficit, the result of a number of simultaneous events. The three academic units that had agreed to experiment with RCM were assured verbally that they would be held harmless for incurring costs necessary to support RCM. Second, a misunderstanding between the administration and the dean over an off-campus lease agreement added more to a debt that exceeded $700,000. The deficit ultimately totaled a million dollars because of expenditures for new technologies made on the assumption that any short-term deficit would be offset in part by revenues from the Educational Leadership Program. But as it turned out, the University of California Office of the President decided that UC's few revenue producing programs like the Educational Leadership Program were to become self-sufficient immediately and that they would now pay a substantial overhead that was earmarked for the administration.

In 1999 the permanent dean, who had been serving as both dean and vice chancellor for planning and budget while an interim dean filled in for him, left to become a vice president at the Getty Museum. Another interim dean took over after the dean's departure (the school had six deans in six years) and was able to reduce the deficit by about $350,000 and helped Center X, which had fallen badly into debt during the expansion years, back to fiscal solvency.

During 1999 new stresses on the university emerged as the regents, responding to Proposition 209 and their own initiatives that banned affirmative action in admissions and hiring, launched new outreach programs to voluntarily develop a pool of qualified applicants that included large proportions of underrepresented students. Much of the financial resources that came to UCLA to initiate new outreach programs fell to the GSE&IS, helping to relieve its budgetary crunch, but also contributing to the pressures on an already overworked faculty. Next, the California governor, responding to pressures to reform public education, launched two additional initiatives aimed at UC (an institute to train school principals and a program to boost the number of teachers trained at the university). Much of this new work came to UCLA and to the GSE&IS that represented new opportunities, but it further exacerbated the faculty's workload and added even more non-core adjunct faculty members to the staff so that the work could be done.

Finally, a new permanent dean took over in the fall of 1999, with the understanding that the remaining deficit be absorbed by the administration. But soon another problem loomed on the horizon. The new membership of the campus-wide committee on academic personnel, the body that passes next-to-final judgments on tenure decisions and other major faculty personnel actions, began to turn down near-unanimous recommendations from their own review committees and the school. In past years, this committee had agreed with the school's mission to integrate theory and practice and developed an expanded view of research that included research that could be applied to solving problems of education while maintaining high academic standards. The new committee on academic personnel, however, took a traditionally conservative view of research and denied some promotions and new hires that had been carefully reviewed and recommended by the school and their own review committees. While a number of cases were overturned on the dean's appeal, this conservative trend began to open old tensions between faculty members who did traditional research that was easily recognized by the committee on academic personnel and those who did more applied work.

References

Stewart, G. R. (1971). *The year of the oath*. New York, NY: Da Copa Press.

The Department of Physics and Astronomy

5

The Department of Physics and Astronomy occupies Knudsen Hall, an older building in the middle of the UCLA campus. It is part of the Division of Physical Sciences in the College of Letters and Science, the largest academic unit at UCLA and home to nearly all undergraduates. The physical sciences division includes four other departments: mathematics, chemistry and biochemistry, atmospheric sciences, and earth and space sciences.

Physics and astronomy is the product of a merger of the Department of Physics and Department of Astronomy that occurred in the mid-1990s as part of the campus-wide strategic consolidation effort. Physics and astronomy is home to 59 ladder faculty members: 44 physicists, 13 astronomers, and two astrophysicists. Also in residence are 24 professional researchers who do not teach but conduct research and 109 staff members. The department offers majors in astronomy, accelerator physics, astrophysics, particle physics, plasma physics, condensed-matter physics, nuclear physics, and low-temperature physics. Almost 130 students are enrolled in PhD programs. The department also offers an undergraduate degree program in which 181 students are enrolled.

Academic Life

Many faculty members in the Department of Physics and Astronomy describe their passion for science as an early calling. For instance, one professor said he had wanted to study physics ever since he became fascinated with experiments in high school. An astronomer said he was drawn to the field as a child when his father took him to the Hayden Planetarium in New York City. Many professors had other similar stories, and what draws them together is a tangible passion, an inner compulsion to become a physicist or astronomer.

Not surprisingly, most professors talk about how they love their work. They cherish the freedom to pursue scientific questions that interest them—a freedom they know they would not find at a national or industrial laboratory. One veteran physicist said, "The big advantage of working in a university environment is that you can do anything you want." An astronomer added:

> To pursue my dream—being able to combine the possibility of exploring the universe, solar system, trying to understand these other phenomena—there is no better place to explore these issues.

Another faculty member admitted, "It's fun, let's face it. If you want a career in life that is as near to play, I think, as anything you can imagine, being a professor is it." Another added, "This is one of the few ways that you can actually spend your life studying and working on the subject you love and someone will pay you for it!"

Most professors say research is the most fulfilling aspect of their jobs. One described what excites him the most:

> I get the most satisfaction out of reaching new understanding, discovering something, figuring out something that nobody had realized before. Sometimes those Eureka moments do happen and fall into place, and you realize you're the first one to have reached that realization. And that's truly exciting. It's like discovering a new valley somewhere that nobody had noticed.

There is a prevailing belief that research should contribute to society's well being and that it should enhance the quality of life, which most professors say they find gratifying. An astronomer said, "As scientists, we play an essential role in modern life by addressing the important issues people need to understand to conceptualize about the world around them." One said passionately, "Once society has learned these things about the universe, they're theirs forever and ever and ever."

Professors' enthusiasm for research is dampened only by the difficulty of getting funding, which many say has become a time-consuming and sometimes frustrating experience. As one explained, "Funding is so tight. I just read that it takes almost 4.2 proposals to get one grant." Making matters worse, funding agencies are pulling back on large grants and awarding smaller ones for shorter periods of time that make life increasingly chaotic for many faculty members.

Most professors say they truly like teaching, but some describe it coldly as a contractual obligation. One professor with this viewpoint elaborated, "You do a certain amount of teaching, and the university allows you to do research." Others say that teaching constrains their research, especially in today's competitive environment. One explained:

> In today's environment, it's so competitive to stay in the research-funding scene that either you're in or you're out. So teaching makes it really hard to stay in the game. So we teach one class every quarter, so there's no break. There's no term that you're off because you're not teaching. So it makes me question how can I stay in at this rate? I mean I'm definitely in now. But I can't keep this up.

But most say they find teaching gratifying. One professor described his role as "helping students appreciate the nature of the physical universe." Faculty members describe the joy they derive from seeing students learn, describing the high point as the "beautiful moment when students get it." One said, "The biggest thrill is being able to be the cause of someone else realizing something very profound and awe inspiring for the first time." Another said:

> Getting undergraduate students excited about
> the material and seeing the light that goes on
> when they really understand that we have a way
> of approaching and understanding nature in
> detail is difficult but very powerful.

Other professors feel enormous responsibility for training
the next generation of researchers, which one likened to parent-
ing. He explained:

> Graduate training is like fatherhood. When peo-
> ple come to you as very bright but not yet capa-
> ble, and when the apprentice exceeds the mas-
> ter's expertise—which happens when these stu-
> dents do their PhD thesis—that's a good feeling.
> You say to yourself, 'Okay, I've created another
> useful member of the scientific community.'

But large undergraduate classes that can be more than 250
students frustrate many faculty members. One professor said
when classes get that large:

> All the students blur together so you can't see
> them as individuals any more. It's hard to com-
> municate because the details get lost. It's hard to
> do deep derivations or complicated problems in
> that kind of an atmosphere.

Another frustration is the growing number of students who
are not well prepared academically. One professor explained
that it was not just the lack of mathematical preparation, but
their lack of maturity and exposure. He continued, "Even after
two years of taking courses they are still not sophisticated nor
prepared to listen to anything modern."

Most professors say they are satisfied with their salaries,
and like faculty members in the Anderson School and the
Graduate School of Education and Information Studies, the
non-monetary aspects of the job far outweigh higher salaries
they might earn on the outside. "It's fine," said one professor

about his pay. "On balance, I think I'm compensated fairly." He added:

> The nonmonetary benefits are enormous. They are probably comparable in size—and people do put dollar terms on these things—to the dollars that we are getting paid, and it's utterly impossible to ignore that.

Another professor replied in a similar way:

> Compensation for my work is largely in terms of personal satisfaction. If I were really concerned about monetary compensation and if I were not satisfied with what the university was giving me, then I really wouldn't have much business being here. I should go out and work in industry where I could double my salary. But then I wouldn't have the same level of satisfaction.

Professors work long hours—10.5 hours each day on average (not counting Fridays, Saturdays, and Sundays). Well over two-fifths of their time (45%) is spent conducting research, while almost a quarter (24%) is spent teaching. About a fifth (17%) of their time is spent involved in service activities. The remainder of their time is split between professional development, mentoring students, and other activities. Faculty members say they spend most of their time on campus (71%). Like their counterparts in the other two units, they also spend a considerable amount of time working away from campus—on average, 16% at home and 13% elsewhere.

The Work of Research and Teaching

Professors in the Department of Physics and Astronomy, as in the other units, say they have several models or types of days—teaching and research days. Administrative duties and public service are blended into both types of days.

Research

A Typical Research Day

A typical research day might begin on campus sometime between 7 a.m. and 9 a.m. After checking email and returning phone calls, physicists might work on proposals or use the computer to analyze data. There is a collegial feel to the place, and colleagues pop in during the day to explore ideas or to get help working out equations on the board. As one professor explained, this way of working is considered optimal intellectual functioning:

> It's not unusual for someone to barge in, not say excuse me, are you busy, but to walk up and be so full of what they're about to say they almost explode. They'll walk up to the blackboard and scribble on it for half an hour and ask my opinion, or maybe just talk about something they've just done and want to vent it. I do the same thing. That's how we all function intellectually.

Special seminars and colloquia are also given frequently to explore new ideas, and faculty members from physics and astronomy attend often.

While most professors do their writing at home so they can concentrate, they analyze their data in their offices on campus. One physicist explained why:

> The best research days are those without time limits that enable us to mull over problems. I can mull on this and put it aside, and then mull on that. And I can pick and choose what I want to think about. This funny synergistic thing, you know, works out better if you can do it in a nonlinear fashion.

The Research Process

The process of research in the Department of Physics and Astronomy varies because of differences in the type of research (theoretical or empirical) and the field (astronomy versus accelerator physics versus plasma physics). Nevertheless, the research process can be organized into six generic steps.

Develop a question. First, some question about a physical problem or phenomenon presents itself for study like a new star formation or a new insight about the behavior of elementary particles. New questions may arise from professors' research, or because of the interdisciplinary nature of physics and astronomy, faculty members may embark on questions that cut across both fields and branch into new areas. For example, one plasma physics professor was working on a project modeling plasma processes when the comet Hyakutake passed the earth and emitted flickering x-rays. Realizing his theories could help explain the flickering, the professor embarked on a new study of x-rays in comets.

Questions of physics and astronomy are often theoretical at first because they are so frequently intangible. Some are infinitesimally small, and others are astronomically large. So theoretical questions are often the starting point for new ideas before they can be tested empirically. For example, one professor's theoretical work in x-rays has spanned more than a decade. Only recently has he been able to test his theories using accelerators at Stanford and the Los Alamos and Livermore laboratories. He explained:

> The goal was to demonstrate or understand the basic physics of the system when an electron beam is produced by an accelerator, a particular type of magnet and electromagnetic radiation. That is, under certain conditions, it would behave in a certain way, which is the way this x-ray laser is based. So there were all these theoretical ideas that developed starting in 1985. Based on those theoretical ideas, you can think of building this x-ray laser, but then you have to prove that these theoretical ideas are logical.

Find funding. Next, funds must be found. Grantsmanship has become a necessary fact of life for astronomers and experimental physicists because they require sophisticated and expensive equipment and instruments like linear accelerators, telescopes and high-speed supercomputers needed to run experiments and analyze data. Most experimental research is supported by federal agencies like the National Aeronautics and Space Administration (NASA), the Department of Energy, and the National Science Foundation (NSF). Grants may range from several thousand dollars to—more typically—several million. Increasingly, proposals are written in collaboration with colleagues at other universities, especially if the project is large (more than $100,000), and proposals usually include support for graduate students.

Astronomers write two types of proposals—money proposals that request funds, and telescope proposals that request access to telescopes, such as Keck and Hubbell to conduct research. Because each telescope has different capabilities, astronomers must often apply to more than one. Professors estimate they spend 10% to 20% of their time writing four proposals that are typically due twice a year. These twice-yearly periods may become particularly hectic. One astronomer described how:

> The telescope proposals are due in September and March, so there's this big push to do this obscene number of proposals at the end of September, like for the Hubbell Space Telescope. So everyone's running around like a chicken with its head cut off.

Prepare for research. A third step is preparation to conduct the research. Preparation is perhaps the most significant phase in the research process because of the need to prepare, and sometimes to actually construct, sophisticated equipment. (In some cases, preparation requires constructing entire labs or building new equipment or components like x-rays and the infrared spectrograph.) Professors must also set up, test, calibrate, and learn to operate instruments like satellites or plasma machines for experimentation. While many of these machines are small enough to fit in a room, they can take months or years to construct and test before they can even be used.

Conduct research. Next is conducting the actual research that can vary greatly depending on whether the research is theoretical or experimental. Theoretical physicists spend much of their time reading, writing, calculating, and constructing theories simply using pencils and paper. Other theorists use computers, often linking to others at the San Diego Supercomputer Center and the Lawrence Livermore National Laboratory. One theorist explained his process:

> I do a lot of reading and writing and a lot of calculating. You know, I sit at my desk with a pen and paper, or at the computer terminal with a keyboard. I don't do experimental work, so I don't have a laboratory or a telescope.

It is a far different story for astronomers and experimental physicists. Depending on their specialty, these scientists may simply go down a few flights of stairs to the basement of Knudsen Hall to use spectrographs, photoinjectors, particle accelerators, or plasma machines. Or they may travel off-site to other universities or to the Collider Detector at Fermilab in Illinois, the Haldron Collider at CERN (a European nuclear research organization) in Switzerland, or the accelerators at the Stanford Linear Accelerator Center or the Los Alamos National Laboratory in New Mexico. Astronomers may use a variety of telescopes like the twin Keck Telescopes in Hawaii, the Lick Telescope owned by the University of California, or privately owned telescopes like those at the Palomar Observatory owned by Caltech.

Collect and analyze data. Collecting data can be intense and exciting for astronomers and experimental physicists. Physicists, for example, may stay at one location such as Fermilab for up to a week collecting data for a plasma experiment. The process of running an accelerator can be equally as intense. One experimental physicist described running an experiment at the CERN laboratory:

> When I'm at CERN it's because the machine is running. The experiment could be running for up

to five and a half months out of the year. During that time the experiment is running 24 hours each day and so we're on shift taking data and trying to fix things if things go wrong.

Similarly, astronomers typically fly to telescopes in other states or countries and after becoming familiar with the instrument, remain as they say, glued to it for several days. During these telescope days, they maximize every minute, sleeping as little as possible and collecting data throughout the night. One astronomer described the experience:

> You sleep like four, five hours before you get up again and you prepare for the next night. It's almost like you're up all night. You eat an early dinner, then you're up until the sun rises, 'til you just can't work anymore. And then you sleep for awhile. And then you get up and you look at the data that you've taken. You try to find out, was this a successful thing to do? Should I do more of this tonight? Should I change my strategy this way or that way? And then you start again at night.

Once back home with the data, analysis begins. Astronomers and experimental physicists may bring back enormous amounts of data that they load onto their own computers or bigger supercomputers. Analyzing these data can be long and laborious as astronomers try to interpret raw images and physicists look for patterns in millions of pieces of data. The process is often very exciting as scientists discover what the data reveal. Professors describe working in bursts during which they may work for more than 24 hours nonstop.

Publish results. In a final step, research findings are published in scholarly journals. Professors often write papers collaboratively with graduate students who work on projects as part of their theses. One professor explained that there is at least one student using the results from every major experiment for his or her thesis. Graduate students are often listed as first author to help their careers. Results are usually presented at national meetings and conferences and then prepared for publication.

Publishing, especially in physics and astronomy, can be a long, drawn out process. Some fields, such as high-energy experimentation, have elaborate review structures that can involve numerous steps and up to 400 colleagues, and take up to six months or more, as one veteran of the process told us:

> There is a long step in which you argue—I should say discuss—the data. First the analysis is given to three other physicists, who look at it carefully. Then the draft—which may be three pages long but have 300 pages of supporting documentation—goes to what we call godparents. They read through the material and make comments to the authors. After the draft gets the assent of the godparents, it is presented to up to 400 people. Then you collect comments from the first draft for two weeks, then prepare a second draft, which is supposed to be relatively polished. The final step is to give a lecture to those people who are interested, and finally it's up to them to give it their okay.

Teaching

A Typical Teaching Day

Unlike research, teaching is more structured. On a typical teaching day, professors may arrive on campus between 8 a.m. and 10 a.m., depending on their teaching schedules. Once in the office, they check email, phone messages, and regular mail that can take from a few minutes to several hours. After checking mail and messages, faculty members begin preparing for the day's class. The amount of time spent preparing for class depends on the professor's familiarity with the class. While some professors write lecture notes the evening before, others wait until just before teaching. They may also prepare problem sets, write exam problems (depending on the week of the quarter), and make copies of class handouts or overhead transparencies.

The Teaching Process

The teaching process varies considerably, depending on the number of times the professor has taught a course, and whether students are undergraduates or graduates. But generally, teaching follows four broad steps.

Initiate course. First, a course must be initiated and justified. Both the physics and astronomy curricula are well-established and defined. Topics are often presented chronologically in the sequence in which they were discovered, one building upon the other. "We build up physics in a sort of historical order," explained one faculty member. "We teach undergraduates as though they were going through time, through 800 years." Another professor explained the necessity of teaching this way:

> It's a relatively old subject that works like a pyramid. You cannot do the next level unless you do the previous one. But not until graduate school, when students have had their basic training, can you finally contemplate covering hot topics.

Physics and astronomy professors have a lot of freedom in choosing what they teach. One professor described how courses are assigned:

> The vice chair sends around a piece of paper listing the courses that need to be taught in the next academic year, and you're supposed to write down which ones you want to do... Most of the time it works itself out that different people want to do different courses, and you get more or less the courses that you want to teach.

The typical teaching load is one class per quarter. However, professors sometimes double up and teach two classes in one quarter to leave the next quarter free for research.

Prepare material. As noted above, physics and astronomy curricula are well-established, and preparing to teach is somewhat routine. Most professors use standard textbooks, many of which have been used for decades. As one professor noted, syllabi for many core courses may remain essentially unchanged for years:

> That syllabus was written probably 25 years ago. There's no reason to change it. Physics doesn't move that quickly. There are the real facts, and those real facts you have to know. There are some people who enjoy teaching a course that is on the edge of research where you can say to the student, 'This is my opinion of what's going to happen,' but there's no opinion for most of us.

A good deal of effort goes into preparing homework problem sets and creating exams that test students' comprehension of material presented in class. Professors complain about the perennial problem of student cheating. They regularly change problems and prepare several versions of exams by scrambling questions to prevent cheating in packed exam rooms.

Teaching a class for the first time requires, on average, 30 or more hours of preparation because of the requirement to create lecture notes, homework sets, and new exams. Preparation time decreases, however, each time the class is taught. Even professors who have taught a course eight or ten times spend one or more hours refreshing their memories before class. One astronomy professor said:

> Regardless of how many times I've given a lecture before, I always worry about it for a few hours, look at my notes again, look at the book, figure out what handouts and problem sets are required... and then, of course, begin to work on making the next exam.

Professors who teach large undergraduate classes typically get help from two or three teaching assistants who lead discussion sections, often hold office hours, and grade homework.

Methods of teaching. After preparing the course, classes start. Most run 50 minutes, three times a week, and some run for 75 minutes, twice a week. Lecture is the standard format, and professors spell out formulas and equations on the chalkboard with little interaction with students. One professor explained:

> It's very important that the students watch me go through the steps on the blackboard. There's an old adage that teaching is information passing from the notes of the instructor to the notes of the student without passing through the brains of either. But seriously, I want them to understand what I did. I never teach with overheads. I never teach with a computer. I never do any of those things because I think that the important thing is the ideas and not the media, especially overheads. If you prepare your course on a computer and project it, you go through the material too fast.

Another described why he preferred the blackboard instead of demonstrations and overhead transparencies.

> I'm a Cro-Magnon... I use a blackboard and a piece of chalk. I may use glossies once in awhile but not for lectures. Most of my colleagues will agree on this. Glossies lead to disaster because you tend to lecture very rapidly and then the students are trying to take notes... Everybody drives everybody crazy. One of the reasons for the chalk and blackboard is that you write at the pace that students write so they can take notes.

Professors try to engage the students or check their understanding of the material with humor, demonstrating concepts like velocity, or by asking questions. One faculty member said of his introductory class, "I try to keep them awake. If you keep them awake, you can teach them something." Another faculty member commented that she uses cartoons on overhead transparencies to get students' attention.

Many professors find lecturing to large classes exhausting. After lecturing for two hours, one professor told a student, "I can't think right now. I'm wiped out." Another told us, "After I come out of class, I'm not about to do research for a couple of hours until I'm decompressed." Teaching is like acting, and it can be exhausting. One professor explained:

> There is that element of being on stage… that element of performance. When you go into the classroom, you're performing for the students. There's a lot of energy being expended, you're pacing backwards and forwards, you're waving your arms around and stuff like that.

Grade students. Finally, professors grade students' work as a way to assess their learning. Professors often standardize the process so they can use help from teaching assistants. One faculty member explained how he does it:

> I have my own FORTRAN programs that I wrote years ago to do grades, long before the data spreadsheet and everything else… When we get a final exam, for instance, it takes awhile to grade. Well I help a lot with the grading because that's one way I can stay in touch with the way the students are learning. But the recording of the scores, the calculation of the final grades, the assignment of the grades, making histograms of the grades, all that I do with FORTRAN… And I wrote them in such a way that I just edit minimal things, type in the grades, and we have it all set up so that by email, we get a class roster. And then I build a FORTRAN program that reads that class roster and puts it in the format that's in the rest of my database.

Professors also hold weekly office hours that range from one to three hours. Attendance depends on the difficulty of a course being taught. Sometimes many students come for extra help, while other times only a few come. In large undergraduate lower-division courses that are required for premedical programs, professors may meet with up to 20 students at a time.

Feedback on the Processes

Feedback on teaching comes in the form of professors' informal observations of students' progress during class and their grades on examinations. Courses are also evaluated using a standard evaluation form, but often it takes months for the results to reach the teaching faculty. We were struck, however, by the closeness that many faculty members develop with their graduate students. Some become their students' mentors for life and advise them on career decisions for many years. This kind of advising also serves as an important form of feedback for professors on the value of their teaching and mentoring.

The Department of Physics and Astronomy produces about 20 new PhDs annually, two-thirds of whom take jobs outside academe. Many find jobs as research scientists in industrial or government labs or as postdoctoral fellows in university laboratories. Some find jobs as what one called glorified computer programmers—and a creative few go to work as traders on Wall Street. Very few graduates—approximately 10% to 20%, according to the chair—become professors. Concrete numbers describing the true destinies of new physics PhDs are difficult to find because at least until now, the department has had no formal tracking system. In the words of the chair, they can just vanish.

Most professors say feedback about their research is indirect and is usually hard to measure. But most say they are proud of their contribution to science and society. One professor explained, using a story:

> Bob Wilson, the gentleman who built Fermilab, was showing someone around the high-energy accelerator. At the end of the tour this person asked Wilson, 'How does what you learn here contribute to the national defense?' Wilson looked at him and said, 'It doesn't. It contributes to making the nation worth defending.'

Even though professors know that some basic research leads to dead ends or to discoveries that will take years to turn into practical applications, most judge their impact in part on helping students satisfy their deep-seated curiosity. A physicist explained:

> It's sometimes hard to say where knowledge leads, but science in general is just seeking knowledge and improved understanding of the world we live in. And from that come applications, and it's just man's natural curiosity of the world around him and what's his place in it, and what's going on.

Astronomers also strongly believe in the contribution that their field makes to society because of its window into the origins of the universe and its destiny. An astronomer elaborated:

> Astronomy is pure research. There are no spin-offs or commercial products. But it is fundamental to human nature because it studies the universe as a whole and where we came from and where we're going. We know that we are made of stellar material. We are literally stardust, made from the exploding stars billions of years ago. And I think that fundamentally ties into human psyche and human curiosity. And so astronomy is very much on the minds of the public. People are really interested in their universe. It almost borders on mysticism.

External Forces for Change

Like the Anderson School and the Graduate School of Education and Information Studies, the Department of Physics and Astronomy is struggling with finding new sources of revenue to offset declining public funds. But this case adds a new set of complex driving forces for us to consider. Much of the growth in physics was fueled by the Cold War. Once it ended, many of the ideas that presented themselves for study became less interesting (and many had already been solved). And because fears of the Soviet Union abated, much of the financial research support from the US Departments of Energy and

Defense began to dry up. At the same time there was a notice-
able decline in student interest in physics as a field of study.

The Glory Days of Physics

Physics professors fondly remember the glory days of
physics—the 40 years following World War II. During the war,
pressure to develop nuclear weaponry created an unprecedented demand for physicists. Physicists garnered unprecedented
levels of support as the federal government poured millions of
dollars into universities, national laboratory facilities, and the
defense industry for basic research. The era of big science was
born. One veteran professor recalled:

> Modern physics really comes from the war.
> World War II changed physics entirely because of
> the huge amount of money that went into the
> atomic bomb and into radar…. That's when big
> science started—after the War, because all kinds
> of money and equipment had gone into it. The
> big minds, nuclear physicist Enrico Fermi and so
> forth, had helped make the atomic bomb and
> radar… Big science started in the 1950s as an out-
> growth of the war. It was already big science, but
> it became huge science.

From the late 1950s through the 1960s, the race to beat the
Soviets who launched the first satellite into orbit added to the
field's growth. A professor explained:

> In the period after World War II, physics became
> the dominant science. It was widely understood
> that scientists who were looking at the cutting
> edge should be supported because in many cases
> they were producing practical applications from
> their work. That way of thinking was replaced by
> the Sputnik era, in which people said we have to
> support science at almost any cost. We have to
> turn out engineers and scientists by the bushel.

As physicists became increasingly visible in the nation's defense effort, the status of physics, particularly in the sciences, shot up. Physicists like Fermi and von Braun were treated like national heroes and many assumed leadership roles. One professor remembers the extraordinary growth of modern physics:

> When I graduated in 1948, physics was still a very minor, backwater field. A year or two later, we were into the postwar period, and physicists who had been involved with radar and nuclear energy went on to become the movers and shakers in all sorts of areas. Physicists were presidents of universities and CEOs of companies. TRW was started by an engineer and a physicist. So there was an extraordinary period during which physics had great achievement, great popularity, and very strong support.

Physics became so popular on university campuses that, according to one professor, it became the target of a phenomenon called physics envy:

> In the 1950s physicists were the dominant people on campus because of this tremendous triumph over relativity and quantum mechanics and then nuclear physics and all the solid-state physics. Physics just seemed to be so successful at explaining the universe, and the intellectual force of the subject was dominating the way people thought to the extent that people in other subjects had physics envy. They wanted their subject to be revered in a similar way.

End of the Cold War

But as the Cold War came to an end in the 1970s, so did the days of big science. No longer in need of high-tech defense weaponry, the federal government scaled back its funding. In turn, public support for physics began to diminish, and its prestige began to fade. Taxpayers began to question the wisdom of spending millions of dollars for basic research that in many cases failed to produce immediate results. Society became disillusioned about the ability of big science to solve America's myriad and complex problems. One professor remembered:

> In the 1950s, everyone thought that science was going to produce this wonderful society in which we'd have lots of free time and everyone would have wonderful care and this, that and the other. Somehow that promise never quite worked out. The poor are still poor and not doing so well. It has led to the dissatisfaction with the idea that science was somehow good for society.

As the public became increasingly disenchanted, physicists began to feel as if they were scapegoats for society's ills. Physics, a faculty member explained, became a "casualty of the Cold War."

While many physicists still consider the field to be vigorous and healthy, others acknowledge the dawning of a new era. One professor said:

> In general, the 20th century has been the century of physics. It is pretty clear that the 21st century will be the century of biology, not physics. Look at the funding of the National Science Foundation, which is about $3 billion per year, and the National Institutes of Health, which is about $12 billion per year. I think there is no question that biology and medicine are going to be the dominant fields of science in the next century.

Not surprisingly, as the halcyon years ended, what was then the Department of Physics began having trouble finding support for research. The department received virtually all of its funding from the federal government as does the combined Department of Physics and Astronomy today—the National Science Foundation (NSF), the Department of Energy (DOE), and the National Aeronautical and Space Administration

(NASA). (The Office of Naval Research [ONR] and the Defense Advanced Research Projects Agency [DARPA] also are important, but play lesser roles.) Recently, federal funding for the Department has remained relatively steady since 1993—about $17 million annually.

But competition for the existing dollars has greatly intensified. A growing number of second-tier universities, many of which had employed the surplus of talented new physics PhDs, began applying for funding. So, while the absolute value of federal research dollars remained constant, there were, according to several professors, more mouths to feed or more pigs at the trough. The chair of physics and astronomy explained:

> The number of people who are competing for funding from the federal government has gone up considerably in the last ten years. Institutions that you would not have thought have pretensions for excellent research actually do—and are now competitors.

The result is that funding is harder and harder to find. Faculty members recognize the tough competition. A plasma physicist said, "Recently there was a call for all plasma physicists to submit proposals to the National Science Foundation. They received 270 proposals and maybe 20 will be funded."

Grant amounts are shrinking too. The chair of physics and astronomy observed, "If we go to agencies like NSF, which typically gave $150,000 or $200,000, we now have a hard time getting $50,000." To continue their research, professors explained, they scramble to obtain funding from multiple sources and cobble them together. A professor explained how it works:

> It used to be that the NSF would fund you annually. You'd write your proposal and get funded about the same time each year. Now, funding is such a difficult challenge that one tends to get small amounts of money from a multitude of sources and it comes in dribs and drabs throughout the year. So the cycle is shattered. And one is

> always pretty much scrambling. Not every-
> body—there are people on stable funding
> because they have long-term projects. That's the
> Golden Fleece—to get on the long-term project
> that will keep you going.

The end of the golden age of physics and growing competition for scarce funds helped produce a gloomy attitude among
many physicists that the big problems have been solved and
major discoveries already made. One professor said, "The
bloom is off the rose. Physics has had a great run for the last 50
years, and I don't see the next 50 years as being anything like
it." The department chair echoed the sentiment:

> The easy plums were gathered long ago. There
> are no longer physics subjects full of discoveries.
> Astronomy is different... You can still make dis-
> coveries, and it's not as pressured. Physicists are
> more aware of their limitations.

Physics professors also note that the problems that remain
are the difficult ones—and more costly to solve. Many of
today's physics problems require more sophisticated and
expensive technology than those of earlier years. Many physicists acknowledge the growing cost, but believe the investment
is needed and feel constrained by reduced financial support. A
theoretical plasma physicist complained:

> We're trying to push frontiers in the subject and
> there is less and less money. And so the field of
> physics in general over the past five or six years
> has gone through a tremendous turmoil because
> of that—a very painful period. Our job is to push
> the frontiers, but we can't do it.

One can sense the frustration of professors who study high-
energy particle physics. One professor who conducts accelera-
tor-based experiments explained the need for more sophisticated technology:

> The nature of what we look at is not getting more
> complicated, but the tools we use have to be more
> and more sophisticated. For example, in my cur-
> rent experiment, we first started colliding beams
> of particles at a rate of 300,000 per second. Now
> we're going up to 3 million per second, and in our
> future experiment in Geneva we'll do 25 million
> per second. So you need faster and faster detec-
> tors to keep up. We're also asking more of each
> measurement... So we need advances in comput-
> ers to keep up with data coming in.

High-energy physics aims to break atoms into pieces of their
subatomic components. These physicists believe that new discoveries hinge on the ability to smash atoms into smaller and
smaller pieces, which requires ever more powerful accelerators,
the cost of which becomes increasingly difficult to justify. One
professor explained:

> In high-energy physics, you have to find much
> more expensive accelerators to get anywhere, to
> do the next round of experiments and take us to
> the next level of understanding. These questions
> are billion-dollar questions in our field. Because
> of that, we are at the limit of what society will tol-
> erate in terms of funding.

In 1993, Congress canceled the superconducting supercol-
lider project in Texas—a symbol of the future of high-energy
physics. The decision attracted national attention. It was killed
because it was considered too expensive and inefficient. Some
physicists say they understood the government's rationale. One
professor predicted that in just a few years it will be possible to
build far more economical colliders that accelerate atoms with
lasers rather than magnets. But, most high-energy physicists
were disheartened by the cancellation that sent the message
that basic physics research was no longer valued.

Cuts in funds for fusion research stand as further proof of
dwindling public support for basic research. For 20 years,

fusion research garnered a large share of federal funding. Committed to the idea that energy could be generated through nuclear reactions, physicists conducted bigger and more expensive experiments. But the experiments failed, and funding for fusion research was cut. "Decades of promises did not come true," the department chair said. "When they failed to deliver, finally somebody noticed."

But not all faculty members have felt the numbing effects of dwindling resources and lack of public interest. For instance, theoretical physicists need relatively little external support to do their work, and astronomers have captured the public imagination. Nevertheless, increasing competition means that professors must write more proposals than ever before to obtain grants. According to the department chair, professors now have to write twice as many proposals each year to get one or two funded, compared to just a few years ago. The amount of time they spend writing proposals has led some professors to wonder whether they can keep up the pace, especially given their teaching responsibilities.

Also, the growing complexity of physics problems and the rising costs of experimentation are driving a subtle trend toward more collaboration in certain fields of physics. One professor said:

> It would be like trying to build an automobile yourself. You need people to provide the necessary expertise. There are so many aspects to making the problem run and getting the data, that you need a critical sized group where there's enough expertise to tackle a big problem.

In high-energy physics, the need for collaboration has increased because of physicists' reliance on increasingly powerful accelerators. Experiments sometimes require 50 to 500 physicists and they can take ten years to complete. Collaborations often include several institutes, labs, or universities. One professor explained how this aspect of the field has grown:

> In the 1950s, a university could afford to have a front-line accelerator, the cyclotron, and they were all over the place. Then in the 1960s they started getting bigger and in the 1970s and 1980s, they outgrew the universities. So now there are just a few national laboratories. I've watched the collaborations that can occur. They are huge things.

Declining Interest in Physics

The declining popularity of physics has not gone unnoticed by potential graduate students who realize that less funding and more competition translates into fewer jobs. One staff member who oversees student admissions explained:

> Word got out that it's not as prestigious an area anymore, that it's much harder to find a job, that salaries have gone, and that people are stuck in sort of ghetto situations of postdoc after postdoc.

Almost half of all new PhDs traditionally have gone into the defense industry, the sector that was hardest hit by the end of the Cold War. One professor explained:

> The end of the Cold War has made a very big difference to the physics department. Our graduates don't walk into automatic jobs anymore. It used to be that UCLA physics graduates got jobs with Hughes. They'd go with McDonnell Douglas. They'd go to Raytheon or Rocketdyne. They'd have jobs in the defense industry or they'd go on to graduate school or whatever. But all those jobs in the defense industry are gone.

Despite the downturn in employment, many physicists take pride in the apparent ability of their graduates to apply their skills in a variety of fields. Many proudly point to a handful of physics PhDs who ended up getting jobs on Wall Street. One explained:

They have the mathematical knowledge that is needed for certain specialized things like trading and pricing derivatives. Or they work as programmers for brokerage firms. They not only have the skills to program, but the analytical skills to formulate the problem.

Physicists attribute their graduates' success to the virtue of a physics education, which many physicists claim teaches people how to think. One professor said:

One of the virtues of a physics education is that you're not trained to be a specialist. Physics is a very powerful education because you learn analysis at a very deep level; you learn engineering, experimental techniques, and computation.

Some physics professors predict that these talents will serve new PhDs well in the future as emphasis on organizational flexibility increases. The chair explained:

In the 1980s, companies tended to hire engineering students—would not touch physics PhDs at all. Engineers come out extremely well trained for technical application. But companies find that their training lasts five years, at which point they become technically obsolete. Whether they have been trained or self-selected, they don't like to change, don't want to pick up new projects. The physics PhDs are trained to be more flexible, open minded, take on different things. Companies have realized that although our graduates are not narrowly trained, they are much more flexible for the long term, more valuable over longer periods of time. This is one of the virtues of a physics education—you're not trained to be a specialist. So you don't have to replicate undergraduate training.

But new PhDs have an increasingly hard time finding academic jobs. The academic market has become tighter for several reasons. First, as one astronomy professor noted, the system of higher education has slowed down after years of growth:

> Graduate education in this country is geared up for continuous growth. If the default is one professor trains a PhD student every few years, universities cannot absorb all those new PhDs. So that's sustainable only if there is an expansion in the number of jobs available in industry.

Second, turnover in the sciences is very low. Many senior people continue to hang onto positions in physics, and unless they are forced to retire, new jobs simply will not open up. In addition, many university deans have been reticent to fill openings when they do arise because of an uncertain future. The result, according to one professor, is that "there has been a wholesale cutback in job opportunities." Another professor said:

> Finding a faculty position is extremely difficult. There are probably only five openings in major universities a year, and each position has probably 200 applicants. So you have to be one out of a hundred to survive after postdoc.

The changing marketplace for physics PhDs is leading the department to consider changing its relatively general graduate curriculum to one that focuses on electricity and magnetism. The chair explained:

> This is a defect of the present structure. We have a view of graduate education developed in the 1930s and 1940s as a way of satisfying demand for technically trained people in the subject. The problem facing the department today is how to change what we do, given the market forces.

The slowdown in physics has taken its toll on the PhD program, which has seen a 36% drop in total enrollment—from 166 students in 1992 to 106 today. The number and quality of graduate applications have also declined each year. In past years, the department admitted between 25 and 30 new PhD students. In recent years, class sizes have held steady at 15 or 20 new students. Declining interest in physics is being felt across the nation, not just at UCLA, as one professor observed:

> The number of students who are going into physics, particularly as a career, has just started to plummet. This trend is not just limited to UCLA's physics and astronomy department; graduate physics enrollment is down by approximately 30% across the nation, in all the major graduate schools.

The continued decline in applications has led some professors to believe a crisis is looming just over the horizon as the best and brightest flee to other fields. One professor explained:

> In my generation it was obvious to a lot of the very bright people that physics is what they wanted to do. But that's not obvious to the present generation. If there's any crisis that's the crisis. Maybe it's only a crisis because I'm a physicist. Maybe it'll turn out that a 100 years from now that there wasn't that much more to learn in physics so all these people not going into physics were doing exactly the right thing and there was no real crisis. But I think there might be a crisis if in fact physics really remains the place where there's an awful lot of action on the international front as regards the study of the structure of the universe and the structure of matter and people don't go into it.

Fewer graduate students mean fewer teaching assistants (TAs). TAs are essential because they teach many of the large classes, lead discussion and quiz sections, grade problems and assignments, post answers to exam questions, and hold office hours. One faculty member admitted, "We have devolved our educational program so that a good deal of the work is done by teaching assistants." A staff member explained further:

> It's considered an incredible burden here at UCLA for the professor who doesn't have enough TAs to deal with everything, who ends up spending hours and hours talking to students, writing problems, grading exams.

The declining number of graduate students also has a profound effect on research. Graduate students are key to a research university's program because they are the source of new ideas, talent, and labor:

> The whole idea of a research university as it differs from a research laboratory is that you have this continual flux of new students coming in, getting trained, making a contribution, and moving on and new people coming in. That is the essential secret ingredient, the secret weapon of universities. In an industrial or even a government research laboratory, the tendency is for people to all grow old together. They hire some new employees, but that is a small effect compared to the influx of students. Students are the key ingredient of the university. If you're getting good students, everything else falls into place. If you're not, there's a problem.

The undergraduate program that offers a Bachelor of Science degree has also shrunk in size from 246 students in 1992 to 181 in 1997. As one professor said, "We see fewer students who are interested in coming to physics—that's part of this anti-science feeling." The department chair added:

> Physics has been under attack since the end of the Cold War. Every student who goes to high school knows that there are shrinking budgets with the cancellation of the superconducting supercollider,

the decline of Bell Labs and AT&T as major industrial enterprises that hire a lot of PhD physicists. In Southern California, of course, is the virtual collapse of the aerospace industry. Students know this; they vote with their feet.

Many of the best students are being drawn to the biological fields that are growing. Another professor observed:

> There is a psychological shift in that my brightest undergraduates want to go more toward biological fields—brain research, microbiology. Biological sciences have risen to preeminence. Physics is further along. It has been a long time since we had Einstein and the advent of nuclear weapons, the Cold War. Those were all things that used to show physical sciences as being for the best and brightest. Now you can get the Nobel Prize in the biological sciences.

Some also speculate that undergraduates are bypassing physics because the style of teaching is regarded as stodgy and boring. In addition, the field has become abstract and removed from practical reality. Unless students are innately drawn to the field, many find little relevance to real life. One professor explained:

> When you talk about elementary particles which are evanescent, last a quadrillionth of a second, and disappear in flashes and have no properties that relate to the things we know, that's difficult to explain to others. We deal with scales that are incredibly short or very long—billions of years or billionths of a second! It's very difficult to grasp those things.

Another professor described the situation a bit more bluntly:

> Most students I know are bored with physics. They can't wait to get out of it. They do like things like the origins of life, the way the uni-

verse formed—the glamorous things. They hate Newton's laws and those pulleys, all the crap you have to do in sophomore physics. Frankly, those things are boring. They go back 200 to 300 years. One thing that is wrong with physics, and the reason it doesn't attract a lot of people, is that it's so traditional. People just can't break out of this mold. If you take a modern physics book, it will contain the same stuff that it did 50 years ago.

Declining State Funding

The Department of Physics and Astronomy, like the Anderson School and the Graduate School of Education and Information Studies, has also had to suffer a decreasing proportion of state funds. Between 1993 and 1998, state funds declined slightly from $9.2 million to $9 million. When adjusted for inflation, this translates into a significant decline in funding. At the same time, the department was unable to generate sufficient external grants to offset the loss in state funding. The chair elaborated:

> In 1983-84, the Department of Physics had a total external grant expenditure of $9.5 million. Astronomy had half a million, so we had a $10 million total. In 1995, we had $12 million together. If you take the smallest inflationary factor—academic salaries—we should have generated $18 million worth. If you take the more realistic inflationary factor of the cost of doing research, we should have generated $22 million to $25 million.

As a result, the department went through a period of downsizing both faculty and staff. Faculty downsizing was achieved through the Voluntary Early Retirement Incentive Program (VERIP) funded by the UCLA retirement systems, as well as some layoffs. Between 1992 and 1997, the number of ladder faculty members dropped from 67 to 58, while the number of professional researchers went from 29 to 24. To cover the teaching load, the department recalled five emeritus professors, bringing the total number of retired professors still working to 23. In addition, five new adjunct professors and lecturers were hired, bringing the total of that group to 11.

While somewhat painful, a hidden benefit of the VERIP was that it provided an incentive for those who were ready to leave. As one faculty member said, "The VERIP situation helped in the sense that people who were sort of marking time left." At the same time, as one faculty member noted, it did not sever ties with those who wished to stay:

> One of the most important people involved in our group is a senior physicist and was a professor at UCLA. He retired taking VERIP III a couple of years ago, but is still very active in research, and he's still teaching. Other than the financial benefits, he certainly didn't leave the university.

Hardest hit was the department's administrative staff. In addition to the budget cutbacks, a new federal directive stipulated that universities could no longer charge secretarial and other support staff to government contracts unless it could be justified. Prior to the directive, the department had pooled state funds and grant monies to meet staff needs. But, under the new directive, staff members who worked on federal grants were to be paid out of university overhead—the university's share of grant money that pays for clerical and other services.

When the directive was implemented, the chair said it was as if a bomb had been dropped in the department. Thirty percent of the support staff was cut, leaving what he called a skeleton crew of secretaries and administrative assistants to run the department. While many professors understood the government's position, they blamed the university bureaucracy for retaining so much overhead money and making it impossible for the department to cover its administrative costs. One professor explained:

> The physics department gets $10 million a year from grant money. Somewhere between a quarter and a half of that money is so-called overhead money, money that goes straight to the universi-

ty, supposedly to be used for secretaries, libraries, etc. Very little of it ever gets back to this department. If we had some control over our overhead money, we could deal with many of the problems that we have. But we can't get it and the university says, 'well why should you be any richer than the humanities, so we're going to take it away and do what we want with it.' The state won't replace it. In fact, half of that overhead goes straight to the state.

Professors say they are caught in a battle between the university and the federal government. One explained:

In the first round, the university abused the support by using research money to run the university. And students are getting support for teaching activities that came out of our grants. Then the federal government said enough is enough, and they pushed back. So the professors are now in between. We're getting it from both ends.

With many support personnel gone, professors vacuum their own offices, type their own letters and proposals, copy their own documents, and manage their own budgets. One described the situation:

We're down to one secretarial person to support six professors, a lot of postdocs, and students. As a consequence, we have to spend a lot of our time just typing up proposals, reading all their regulations—and that's not cost effective. But it never shows up on anybody's bottom line that they're paying me to do secretary's work, when a secretary is much more efficient at it than I am, and I earn much more than a secretary!

Perhaps even more important, the lack of administrative support cuts deeply into recruitment that in turn hurts the department's future. One professor explained:

I'm on the admissions committee. One of the reasons our admissions process went awry in the past few years was that there weren't enough people keeping an eye on it. There used to be three full-time employees who kept track of that. They did a great job when it came time to send out application materials, receive applications, process them, tell us when things were wrong. Now we have two part-time people doing it. That really showed. I was shocked.

Scarcity of administrative support appeared to exact a substantial toll on some professors, one of whom said:

As a consequence, the infrastructure has disappeared, and we are close to the breaking point. We haven't gotten to the bottom, but we're getting close to it. I mean a lot of people are questioning whether it's worth continuing here. They are getting really frustrated.

Without new funds, the physical infrastructure of Knudson Hall that houses the Department of Physics and Astronomy, also has suffered. Built in the late 1950s, the building's primary function was to be a research facility, and as such, it was outfitted with only the basics, like power and water. Today, faculty members complain about broken seats, lack of blackboards, and outdated equipment. The laboratories are a particularly sore spot. The chair explained:

You can walk into any junior college and find better laboratory resources. We are embarrassed to take people into our labs. We have not had a dime for instruction equipment in 15 years. How can we provide a high-quality education when we can't have a competitive lab? We try, we squeeze money out of the budget. But we're struggling.

Another professor elaborated:

> We use conventional optical telescopes when electron microscopes became the standard 30 years ago. We have a $2 million facility—the Keck Isotope facility—two floors down, provided by a philanthropic organization. And yet the other laboratory equipment our students have available is pre-Sputnik.

The general discontentment stems from the perception that the university has not maintained the building. The chair said, "Other universities would tear down buildings like this. In the last 20 years we have not received a nickel of instructional funds."

A Tightening Downward Spiral

Unlike other physics departments, UCLA's lacks a high-profile research facility that many believe would help attract top faculty and graduate students and enable it to capture more funding. For historical reasons, UCLA decided against creating Organized Research Units (ORUs) to house large projects in favor of a more fluid, multidisciplinary approach to research. According to many faculty members, that decision has hurt the department in today's competitive world. "The challenge," said one faculty member, "is figuring out how to remain a top department when we don't have the research infrastructure that top departments already have."

Some professors blame the university administration for not championing big science projects. One physics professor complained:

> Unfortunately, our administrators have been helpful, but that's not good enough... In today's climate, it requires more active participation by the administration to get projects funded and brought here. So we try for smaller things because the smaller things then don't depend so much on administrative support. But smaller things don't build infrastructure. They're just maintenance of what you have.

An astronomy professor elaborated on the point saying:

> If the university had its own telescope—that's a facility that astronomers will bind around, protect, get resources for... If ten faculty members stand up and ask for a new widget for this telescope, they have a much better chance than if one asks. In condensed-matter physics, a whole area of high-tech is associated with development and construction of materials. Some have immediate applications—can create whole new industries, like silicon chips. We have none of that in this department. We could never fabricate a material here. If we had that, it could involve the research of five or six faculty members. Instead, if our faculty has a new sample of material to study, we have to go elsewhere because such a material could not be produced here. If Bell Labs creates new material, they are not going to give it to us. So we get junk that other people produce, which means we are not competitive.

But other professors and the chair were not so sanguine. The chair explained:

> I would actually be leery of going down that road. Today, one needs to be fluid, able to change quickly because interests of the government change quickly. They have yet to establish at what level they want to support science as part of national policy. Until they settle on that, it would be foolish to set up a rigid structure. Our problem is that we have a rigid departmental structure.

As it became evident that the administration would not support a large-scale research infrastructure, the department began to hire entrepreneurial faculty members who could generate research support on their own. The chair explained how this strategy worked in times of growth, but today an entrepreneurial faculty is a liability:

> We hired people who had the psychology of each running his or her own group, forming his or her own program independent of the existence of anyone else because there wasn't anything in common held by the department that mattered very much to them. When research funding was plentiful, this was a reasonable response to the fact that the university was not going to invest in a major facility that would unify faculty. But we have continued to operate and hire faculty in this mode through periods when the whole funding situation has changed.

Most faculty members agree that the lack of research infrastructure has hurt the department's ranking. Since the 1970s it has been ranked 15th where it has hovered (plus or minus a few points). While a low ranking does not have as direct or dire consequences in physics and astronomy as it does at the Anderson School, most professors say it hurts indirectly. One explained:

> It's the perception of the department that makes a big difference to people who apply. We're ranked 15th, which is not very good. It means that we lose people to Stanford, so we're really scraping the bottom of the barrel.

Some professors voiced concern about the ramifications of being stuck in the second tier. One told us:

> Maintaining the reputation and trying to improve it is hard. With a good reputation comes better students, better prospects for funding, a more attractive place for new faculty. So reputation is very important. You raise the department's reputation by doing good research and hiring in areas where exciting things are going on.

An astronomer elaborated:

> Let's say you are a funding agency in Washington. You can only fund a certain number of people. They're going to say, 'Well, I think we should fund the best places.' Then it becomes self-perpetuating. If you don't have the best reputation, and you become everybody's second choice, you can lose out. It goes both ways. The rich get richer, and the poor get poorer. In this case, in academic life, it's a competition. So that is a struggle.

There was little evidence that the faculty was truly concerned about being ranked in the second tier. Some say it is because of inertia that has developed over the years—the department has never ranked in the top tier and it hasn't sufficient control over its own destiny to change it.

The Department Responds

To characterize the changes that began in the early 1990s, a departmental response would be to mistake what really happened. The Department of Physics (as it was in 1993) found itself unable to act, paralyzed by a sense of complacency left over from its halcyon years. This paralysis was made worse by a pervasive feeling among faculty members that they had little or no control over the destiny of their department. Making matters even more difficult, most of the faculty was senior, tenured and protected. Most faculty members tried to ignore the warning signs for as long as possible. It was a dangerous set of circumstances that caught the department unprepared for what was about to happen. As we shall see, what occurred over nearly a decade happened sporadically. Most of the changes were not what could be called strategic, rather they were reactions to forces that could be ignored no longer. Some changes came from the outside, others from within. But as hit-or-miss as these responses were, they added up to a winning combination that appears to have put the department on a solid footing.

The Introduction of Responsibility Center Management

In 1993, the Division of Physical Sciences in the College of Letters and Science, which included the Department of Physics, volunteered as one of three campus units to implement Responsibility Center Management (RCM) on an experimental basis. But it soon became clear that RCM, which promised to make financial and academic decision making more transparent, had failed to have any impact on the faculty. A staff member recalled:

> I had an idea of how it was supposed to work, but I didn't have a clue of how it was going to change or impact this department or my job. I was not told that yes it's in place and now you're accountable for this number of square feet, and if you don't bring in this kind of money, the footage will be taken away from you, or you're going to be charged.

One reason that RCM was not well understood was because it was introduced at the divisional level, rather at the department level. Another staff member explained:

> RCM is totally theoretical because RCM in this case is the college. It may have something to do with the business school versus the education school versus the college or something like that.

He said he thought that RCM might cause some administrative changes, but noted that his bosses did not expect anything radical. He added, "The college has frequently said they're pretty much going to keep on doing things the way they always did."

Only few professors at the department level had even heard about RCM. They said they thought it had something to do with the structure of finances but little more. One professor, worried that RCM was like "the camel's nose in the tent." He elaborated:

I'm beginning to see it. It's just starting. It used to be that you were assigned to a place and you do your research there. If the funding slackened, you still kept your space. Now, if the funding goes away, you may lose the space. Also, I am constantly questioned about how much it will cost to move my machinery and equipment around. In the beginning, I just had to provide an estimate, a ballpark estimate. Now it gets into more and more detail. I have to account for all utilities in terms of dollars. How much does it cost to have a crane or a truck moving this and that—reconstruction, technicians, labor, and all these things.

But, as we discussed earlier, while RCM was perfectly attuned to the businesslike Anderson School, it failed to have much impact on the academic programs in either Physical Sciences or the Graduate School of Education. The faculty sensed RCM's potential to make academic decision-making more transparent, and they quietly closed ranks, rejecting the idea, causing it to wither.

The Merger

The following year in 1994, the Department of Physics merged with the Department of Astronomy to form the Department of Physics and Astronomy. While the merger was driven primarily to cut costs, there was a natural affinity between the two departments. Physics wished to develop a stronger presence in astrophysics, and the merger enabled a new joint program in cosmology to be quickly developed. The former chair of the astronomy department explained:

There's really no intellectual sense in separating physics, astrophysics, and astronomy. We all recognize that, and we're glad that we can now draw upon a greater pool of knowledge.

Initially, the idea of a merger caused some trepidation on both sides. Astronomy's worry stemmed from the size differential—the Department of Astronomy had only a dozen faculty members and 25 students, compared to Physics' 50 faculty members and 125 students. Astronomers were worried about being swallowed up by the larger department. The physicists, quietly wondered if the astronomers could match their level of excellence.

Industry Partnerships

In 1996, the new Department of Physics and Astronomy tried to establish some new partnerships with industry to offset decreasing support for basic research and the increased emphasis on applied science. While some professors described how partnerships with industry were common in the past, they proved harder to establish in today's climate because industry's focus has become so short term. The chair explained:

> If you go back 20 or 30 years, there were much closer ties between faculty and industry. As industry became much more focused on short-term research—research from financial objectives—they became less interested in having people around who took a broader view of what research is all about. When they come to you with a specific question, when they get the answer they go away. They're not really interested in a long-term relationship.

Another professor was blunt in his criticism of industry partnerships. He said that working closely with industry is dangerous because the "short-term philosophy that permeates industry will infect the university like a virus." He was convinced that the only viable source of funding for long-term research is the federal government:

> If long-range research does not go on in the university, it won't go on anywhere because you

> have to pay for it somehow. In modern times, the
> fruits of long-term research fall very far from the
> tree—outside the boundaries of any particular
> company or even any particular industry. So the
> only sensible way to support them is the federal
> government. An individual company, or even an
> industry, will only support those things that are
> short-ranged by necessity of our economic sys-
> tem. If long-range things are not supported by
> the government, they won't be supported by any-
> one. And if they are not supported by anyone, we
> shortly will have no seed corn.

Another difficulty proved to be how to determine intellectual property rights and patents. One faculty member noted,
"There are all kinds of problems with proprietary rights that get
the lawyers involved. And once the lawyers show up, you can
forget it." Several professors admitted they had little experience
with property rights and patents, and that UCLA's Office of
Sponsored Research is not particularly helpful.

The few partnerships that were developed tended to wither
away. "Of the few faculty members who have tried to establish
relationships with private industry," said the chair, "nothing
came of it." Some think the lack of success stems from the lack
of university infrastructure to support it. One professor who
attempted to develop a partnership acknowledged, "We just
don't seem to have the infrastructure, and so it seems to work
very awkwardly. We have some meetings—there is a lot of heat,
but not much happens!"

Professors say that partnerships with industry seem to be
much more successful in the engineering field. According to
the chair, "It's particularly hard for us on the College of Letters
and Science side because the industrial connections that were
the most naturally established were with the School of
Engineering. Engineers," explained the chair, are more "application oriented and understand the language, the give and
take, and the needs of private industry." But professors of
physics and astronomy say they have found it difficult to

establish relationships with engineering because of a long-standing lack of cooperation.

Faculty Inertia

As attempts to respond to the changing environment continued, it became apparent that faculty inertia—born of the reasons discussed earlier—was a tangible obstacle. This could be seen best around the department's low national ranking. There was the palpable sense that improving the department's ranking would require substantial changes over which the department had little control, like hiring more professors in new fields, or faculty stars to lead new initiatives. One faculty member even said the department lacked control over students' evaluations:

> It would be nice to improve our ranking because it's pretty important, but there is a certain amount of inertia here. The actual things that we could do to change the way departments are evaluated by the grad students and postdocs and so on... there's not much we can do about that.

Inertia also seemed to stem from a tradition of faculty collegiality that also makes it difficult to surface and resolve conflicts. One professor said the faculty was simply "too nice" to each other. He elaborated:

> Why have CalTech, Berkeley, and Stanford continued to be in the forefront while UCLA tries to play catch-up? I think part of it is that we're a bunch of good guys. We're too kind for our own good. I don't want to belittle my colleagues—I probably fall in the same category as the rest of them. But the problems are, if somebody is doing good work, do you encourage good work or do you say no, let's shoot for somebody who is absolutely superb? That's a tough decision to make because you sit and work with colleagues

all the time—it's like telling your brother or sister,
I'm sorry, but...

In the end, it was the very real threat of extinction that pen-
etrated the faculty consciousness and galvanized them into
action. Unless the department could find new resources to offset those that were steadily being lost, the results could be cata-
clysmic. For the first time in 1996, the faculty came to the
painful realization that the department had to pursue new
directions to ensure its future. Within months, faculty members
began talking openly and sincerely about what these new directions might be. One faculty member said:

> I go to meetings now where we discuss whether
> it's a sensible thing to go into biophysics or astro-
> physics. Should we do it in a big way or in a
> small way? Should we still study nuclear
> physics? It's an old-fashioned subject. These are
> difficult questions.

The chair, a quiet but persistent man, knew that the department had to begin thinking strategically rather than simply
reacting to changes. By 1997 he was obviously pleased with the
increased consciousness of the faculty. He said:

> For the first time ever since I've been around, the
> department is consciously trying to understand
> where it wants to go. We sit in a state where as
> you look up and down the coast, you see institu-
> tions of higher learning that are powerful play-
> ers. It's a very competitive environment and
> you've got to decide whether you want to com-
> pete head-on with some of those, or do you want
> to try to develop areas of expertise which are
> complementary but nevertheless stake out a
> unique identity for UCLA in this consortium of
> powerful universities. Those are some decisions
> that we don't want to rush into.

Consequences and More Change

New Academic Programs

One of the first victories in this new state of mind was the establishment of the infrared laboratory. The ability to detect infrared light enables astronomers to see to the very edge of the universe and detect distant galaxies that would otherwise be invisible. In recent years, the department recruited two faculty members to build infrared instruments for the Keck telescope in Hawaii, the world's largest telescope—which is operated jointly by the University of California and Caltech. Members of the astronomy faculty teamed up to build state-of-the-art infrared equipment. One astronomer explained:

> A lot of astronomers just observe things. They don't build things. They go use somebody else's infrared camera for the Keck telescope. But here, we're building our own infrared cameras, and have very quickly become possibly the best infrared laboratory in the world, at least in the United States, for actually assembling, putting together pieces of equipment. They have millions of dollars worth of grants now—it's a high-growth area—partially because, and this is something we recognized in the beginning, we are building hardware.

Another achievement was the establishment of a new field of biophysics, the application of physics to biological problems. As one professor explained, applying physics to biological problems may make it finally possible to understand problems about life that biology alone cannot answer. While a new program in biophysics is not unique (Princeton and UC Berkeley are establishing their own), it was chosen as a promising area because, according to one professor, "it represented a field that was actually growing."

New Graduate Student Recruiting

Faced with a potential shortage of PhD students, the department responded by stepping up recruitment efforts. Faculty members make personal phone calls to prospective students, staff members send out hundreds of applications and promotional brochures, and the department began holding a recruitment day. Despite more aggressive recruiting, there may be a limit to its success because many students are simply not interested in physics. One professor explained:

> That's not something you can effect. You can put more effort into recruiting, you can go out and more actively recruit students from the undergraduate schools or at the undergraduate levels from the high schools, but I don't think there is much you can do about it. It's like trying to change the weather.

The faculty has discussed the wisdom of lowering standards for admission to maintain the enrollments it needs. While most professors dislike the idea, it may become inevitable. As one explained, "With the shrinking pool, your few elite universities snatch up the top people, so it just makes it more difficult." Indeed, the average score on the Graduate Record Examination dropped from 754 to 724 over the past six years.

An alternative approach is to seek students with atypical backgrounds. In the past few years, the department has begun admitting students from smaller schools, a strategy that had been avoided because students from small colleges were unprepared for UCLA's large size and competitive environment. One admissions officer explained:

> We've found that even A+ students from smaller schools, where they haven't gotten the range of physics opportunities as far as research and undergraduate courses, have trouble adjusting to UCLA. So in the past we've been very leery about taking too many students from small schools

because they get here and die, and we don't like to see that happen.

Another option is to admit a higher number of foreign students. A major drawback is the high costs because foreign students cannot become residents, and must pay the significantly higher out-of-state tuition. The department can defray the cost for about seven foreign students per year, but no more. Moreover, the steady supply of foreign students may be declining as well. One staff member explained:

> Traditionally, the assumption was that slots would be filled by foreign students; however, this is no longer the case. At one point, physics was attracting the best and the brightest students not just from here but from all over the world—from China, Russia, and so on. And now in China it's not as prestigious to come to the United States and study. It's much more prestigious to go into business in China. The luster is off with the decline of employment.

Impact of the Merger

By 1998, the merger appeared to be paying off. An astronomer described the natural synergy between the two departments:

> We have a natural kinship with physics, and it's natural for us to merge with them in terms of our intellectual commonalties. It has positively affected us because it broadens our horizons. Physicists work in ways that we need to learn to think in, in order to do things a bit better. And vice versa, once in awhile! Neither is better, because the nature of the sciences is different. The astronomer never gets to handle the objects of his or her study. We almost do more passive studies than in physics, where you can tweak and poke and scratch the things you're working on.

A definite positive outcome of the merger became the development of a small number of subfields that combine the two disciplines, all of which fall generally under the area of astrophysics. One example is astroparticle physics, which is an overlap of high-energy particle physics and astronomy. The chair described how working together has improved camaraderie between faculty members:

> This is the first time we have had real movement together between the high-energy physicists on the one hand and the astronomers on the other, to do this. And, we're beginning to see high-energy physicists wanting to go over and teach Astronomy 3, which is the general education course in astronomy. It happened for the first time this year. They volunteered to do it. They wanted to learn the bread and butter of astronomy. It's a wonderful experience. So they're beginning to do that. And at the same time, people from astronomy are starting to come over and want to teach physics lab. So it's beginning to pull together in a rather interesting and nice way.

An astronomer described the inevitability of a closer alignment with physics:

> Astronomy is an older science than physics. In fact it's the first physical science. Astronomy is the first place where people saw order in nature... And now astronomers routinely use physics in everything they do. Today, astronomy is really astrophysics, and the two are inseparable. The word *astrophysics* cannot be distinguished from astronomy in modern science. And therefore, we are as much of a branch of physics as solid-state physics, plasma physics, or nuclear physics. These branches are all as different from each other as we are from any one of them. So

we're just now part of this larger umbrella. It makes a lot of sense. Intellectually, it's better because now that we're a single department, there are initiatives underway to talk to each other and hear what our colleagues who are a bit further up field are doing. That's been good.

So far, the only potential drawback was that the two former departments still occupy their original space in separate buildings, making administration difficult.

Modernization of Undergraduate Major

Complaints that the physics curriculum was too hard, there were too many required courses, and that students could not take enough electives, prompted the department to reorganize the physics major. Another reason was the realization that few undergraduate physics majors—perhaps as few as 20%—were electing to pursue graduate work in physics. Instead, they opted for law or medical school. The department decided to eliminate the first eight weeks of the physics curriculum and cut the number of required physics classes from five to three, allowing more room for physics majors to take electives. The chair explained:

> We finally had to face the fact that at the undergraduate level, 80% of our physics majors go off and do something else than go to graduate school in physics. So we wanted to allow them the opportunity to take other courses. We had locked up courses to the degree that they didn't have time to take anything else. So we tore up the plan we had for their senior year, which used to be only physics-based electives, and said students could create their own plan that made sense. Now students can go off to take a coherent curriculum in another department, and we are happy to accept it. It's too early to tell how significant it will be. But again, it was a response to

the fact that we saw our customers not being well served.

To compensate for the eight weeks of physics that students now do not have to take, the department tells potential physics majors that they must pass a qualifying examination that is posted on the department's web page. If students fail the qualifying examination, they must take a web-based independent study course worth one credit to bring them up to speed. They can then retake the qualifying exam, and if they pass, they are admitted to the physics major.

The reorganization of the undergraduate major was also a response to UCLA's new and more stringent fiscal environment that grew out of the RCM initiative. One staff member explained:

> The university has changed its accounting structure and the way departments get money from the deans. That is more than a simple decision about bookkeeping. It basically says to the departments, your students are clients in a way, you know, customers. The more customers you have, the more money you're going to get, because the departments get money based on how many seats they fill. It's like a business. So now you have to worry about how many students are moving through your program because your departmental money is being tied to that directly.

Marketing Physics Courses

Budget constraints also led the department to tailor its courses to students' needs more than ever before. Ninety percent of physics and astronomy undergraduate courses are service courses that enroll about 2,000 nonphysics majors each year. These students, who are majoring in subjects like chemistry, engineering, and life sciences each require a three-quarter physics sequence. About half the nonphysics majors are in a premedical program. In the past, these sequences were essentially a diluted version of what the physics faculty taught its own undergraduates. Despite the fact that courses were simplified, premed students, feeling pressured for high grades, continued to dread physics courses because they were difficult and posed a risk to the grade-point averages. The medical school approved of these tough physics courses because they served to weed out marginal students. A physics staff member explained:

> In the past, the medical school didn't care so much because they used physics as a washout class. They wanted physics to be so hard that med students who didn't get an A in physics had no chance of going on... in other words, to weed them out. It was viewed as a bottleneck. That put tremendous pressure on med students when they took physics. They were frantic to get an A and didn't care if they learned anything. They just viewed physics as a hurdle. It didn't matter what the material was. So how do you think they evaluated the class when they wrote their evaluations? They'd say, 'This is the hardest class I ever took. I hate physics. I hope never to learn it, it's totally irrelevant.'

All of this changed when the medical school began paying attention to how students evaluated teaching. The staff member continued:

> In the past, the med school didn't care about it. Now things are different. I don't know whether the economy for doctors has changed, but now they're saying, 'Well, our students aren't giving you good evaluations. You'd better improve if you want to keep teaching med students.'

The medical school backed up its demands by threatening to offer its own physics courses. A staff member remembered:

The dean of the medical school basically said, 'If you don't do a better job teaching doctors what doctors want to know, we're going to teach physics to the doctors ourselves. We won't require them to take physics from the physics department. We'll require them to take a class from the medical school.'

Because funds are allocated on the basis of students, the Department of Physics and Astronomy knew that the medical school would benefit from teaching physics. The potential loss of medical students represented an enormous threat to the department—especially because of the low number of physics majors. The physics and astronomy faculty began to realize that it was essentially being subsidized by the medical students. The staff member explained:

If the physics department loses the medical students, then graduate physics operates at a loss because there aren't that many graduate physics students. You can't support all the faculty if they're being paid by graduate physics.

Eventually, the department responded. The chair's comment revealed a significant change in attitude:

We haven't paid much attention to the fact that we have customers. This is part of the change that is beginning to happen to physics—the realization that there are different customers.

Since then, the department created and tested a new biophysics curriculum. The chair explained:

We decided that teaching students how balls roll down planes was not what they were interested in if they were going into the life sciences. So one of our faculty designed an entirely new curriculum that teaches physics that life scientists want to know—muscles, charges in and out of cells.

> They've designed an entirely new course and are trying out new labs and experiments. And they've written texts. This is, in essence, a response to our customers. They've tried it for one year—and the customer is pretty happy.

The new curriculum generated some controversy among the traditional physicists because it departed so strikingly from what they recognized as pure physics. A staff member observed:

> It's not the physicists' conception of physics. It's biophysics. No principles or laws of physics are taught unless they're relevant to the biophysics of the human body. There are some very important concepts in physics—like Faraday's Law, for instance—that are not important for the body. These are not even touched. These are major, major changes. Physicists themselves are divided over whether it should be taught this way or not.

In addition, the department has created a second tier of classes that are as rigorous as physics courses for physics majors. The strategy represents a concerted effort to recapture the bright students who are now being drawn to biology and medicine. A veteran physicist explained:

> This may be arrogance, but physicists believe that in the past, they have attracted the very best people to their field. So we are now trying to devise a program that will attract those people who, 20 years ago, would have been attracted to physics. We will still teach them academic physics, but point them toward a biology career. So we'll once again attract the very best people, plus the strength of their physics training will make it easier for them to succeed in biology or for that matter, other fields that they might go into outside of academic physics. So this second part of the biophysics curriculum will be as rigorous and quan-

titative—full of mathematics and so on—as our standard physics curriculum. But it will go beyond the bounds of our standard academic curriculum, because that standard academic curriculum only leads to jobs in areas where the funding is poor and jobs are few.

While the trend toward customizing physics is occurring, it is moving slowly. One of the professors who created the biophysics curriculum observed:

Teaching is becoming a more important part of the service to the university. We used to think that basically what we want to do is to create a new generation of physicists. Now we are not making new physicists. Rather, we are educating students in a different field. Not very many professors in the physics department appreciate or recognize that transition.

Summary

Professors in the Department of Physics and Astronomy are passionate about their research, and they appreciate the university environment that affords them the freedom to pursue their research. Most find teaching gratifying although, along with administrative duties, the teaching is viewed by some as an intrusion on their research.

Typical Day

Faculty members work an average of 11 hours each day, most of which is divided between research and teaching. The actual process of conducting research begins with a question—a desire to understand some physical problem or phenomenon. The process is often resource intensive because the technology needed to gather data and conduct experiments is sophisticated and expensive. Most research support comes from federal sources, and faculty members say they spend more and more time writing proposals because of limited funds and increasing competition. Professors describe their research as intensive and arduous, but it is always exciting. Experiments often lead to scientific discoveries that typically are published in scholarly and professional journals. Scientists often work collaboratively on experiments, and joint publications are common.

Curriculum

Rooted in the history of science, the physics and astronomy curriculum is considered fundamental knowledge and is taught in a manner that has changed little over the years. Basic courses are relatively standardized and taught in large lecture halls, usually with the assistance of graduate student teaching assistants. Most professors shun classroom technology found in other units like the Anderson School and use lectures with chalk and blackboards to illustrate formulas and ideas. Professors say their greatest challenge is transferring their excitement about physics and astronomy to their undergraduate students and developing their ability to think deeply and critically. Graduate training is more akin to the traditional apprenticeship in which motivated students work alongside their mentors in a collaborative way, usually publishing together.

Changes

Despite its deep and historic roots, physics and astronomy has recently undergone profound changes that reflect the evolution of the fields and the department's changing operating environment. The end of the Cold War and public disillusionment with physics led to a loss of prestige that has not been regained. Increasing competition for a fixed amount of federal dollars has forced faculty members to write more and more proposals that bring in smaller and smaller grants. At the same time, research problems have become more complex and require increasingly sophisticated and expensive technology to solve. Fewer job opportunities for physicists following graduation have translated into declining interest in both the undergraduate and graduate programs. The latter has a special impact on the department because of the valuable assistance graduate students provide to faculty teaching and research. The department's long-term viability has been further threatened by the growth of biology and subsequent emigration of students to fields like brain research and microbiology.

Simultaneously, decreased state funding led to a series of painful reductions of both faculty and staff. Added to the lack of university investment in upgrading the department's infrastructure, the administrative cuts exacted a toll on departmental morale. And to date, there has been little response to faculty wishes for assistance from university-level administrators to foster multidisciplinary research opportunities and an infrastructure that would enable organized research.

But once the faculty finally became aware of the serious threats to their department's long-term survival, they became energized and engaged in informal strategic planning. The result was a number of new initiatives related to both research and teaching aimed to ensure the department's survival and growth. In 1994, the Department of Physics merged with the Department of Astronomy in an alliance designed to move the new department toward the growing fields of astrophysics and cosmology. The physics and astronomy department also developed a new biophysics program designed to attract good students who otherwise might choose biology or another life-science major. And the department has stepped up its student recruitment efforts. Various other initiatives have produced gains in external funding and increased status, including an infrared laboratory, which builds key components for the Keck telescope. In a radical departure from the past, the department has modernized the physics major to attract more undergraduates. The medical school's threat to offer its own physics classes was instrumental in forcing the department to develop a series of customized service courses for non-physics majors, like students of chemistry, engineering, and the life sciences, who must take a physics sequence to fulfill their majors.

Addendum: From Late 1998 to 2001

Since late 1998 the Department of Physics and Astronomy has continued to respond successfully to changes in the environment. According to the chair, faculty morale has improved substantially as the financial picture has begun to improve. In 2000, the department brought in $17.6 million in external funding—substantially more than the $11 million obtained in 1996 and more than double the $8 million secured in 1992.

The department has also continued to explore new growth fields. As many of the faculty expected, biophysics has indeed emerged as a new frontier in science, and the department's commitment to invest has increased. Entry has been difficult, however, because the department has had to compete with well-endowed private universities for the few stars who are only now being produced by top-tier institutions. Despite the stiff competition, the department recently hired its first biophysicist. In hopes of defining a unique niche for itself, the department is adopting a two-pronged strategy that focuses on both biophysics and on the use of nanotechnology to develop microscopic but nonbiological structures that mimic those being discovered in the biological realm. The department has also hired its first professor of string theory, a new field that may close the gap between particle theory and general relativity. Astronomy is, in the words of the chair, still booming and continues to enjoy strong public support. The department has also hired an expert in astroparticle physics, a field that enables scientists to explore the early universe by measuring the radiation of particles at the highest energies that nature can produce. The hope is that with the merger of physics and astronomy the new department will emerge as the leader in this field.

Progress has also been made in developing government and industry partnerships and collaborations. The department's infrared laboratory successfully delivered its first instrument to the Keck telescope. Soon after, the infrared lab was awarded a $3.3 million contract to build additional instruments for Keck, including a telescope to be attached to the side of a Boeing 747. The department is also part of a large joint effort among more than a dozen academic institutions and government laboratories to simulate controlled fusion. Funding from this project has enabled the creation of a one-of-a-kind instrument in UCLA's new science and technology building that is fueling a revival in plasma physics, an area considered to have been in the doldrums.

A new organized research unit arrived on the horizon as well. In 2000, the department collaborated with the School of Engineering, the School of Medicine, and UC Santa Barbara on a proposal to establish a major research center. The proposal was a success. In 2001 the department formed the California NanoSystems Institute which will receive $100 billion over a four-year period, providing valuable capital investment for the department's venture into nano-scale science.

Improvements have been made to the department's curricula as well. The strategy of providing customized service courses for life science majors has gained acceptance among physics faculty and is now considered a success. Tailored courses for engineering and other physical sciences are being developed as well. At the graduate level, the curriculum has been streamlined, allowing the department to accept more foreign students—who now account for 50-80% of graduate physics programs in private universities. (Foreign students now take the advancement to candidacy examination earlier in their program, reducing the time the department must pay their out-of-state tuition.) Next, the department plans to modernize the graduate curriculum to better reflect the evolution underway in the field.

6

Managing Change

The cases we have just examined reveal the vast changes that are sweeping across the landscape of higher education. Eroding public support for higher education, increased competition for students and scarce dollars, new technologies that are reshaping universities' teaching cores, and pressures for privatization are pushing these dignified organizations' structures and cultures to their limits. Do colleges have to wait for disaster to strike before they can change? Or can they learn to manage change in a planful way? What can be learned from the cases we have just examined?

It is obvious that although managing change has become a cliché, academic leaders ignore it at their own peril. Each of the cases makes clear just how difficult it is to alter an institution's course in the midst of uncertainty. The Anderson School leadership responded quickly to the loss of public resources by offering new, high-priced MBA and Executive Education programs to generate new revenue. But it misjudged the consequences of trying to raise the school's *Business Week* rankings that had slipped badly by dumbing down courses and making students happier customers. The consequence was a rebellion among the senior faculty who asserted their authority and insisted on educational quality being the priority. But the competing pressures for scholarly research and high quality teaching did not abate. In response, some professors began to specialize in teaching, while others decided to concentrate on research. The result of these changes (that still remain unresolved) is the fear among faculty members that Anderson will split into two camps: One of excellent teachers without academic research credentials, and the other of excellent researchers who are not necessarily good teachers.

The Graduate School of Education and Information Studies was fortunate because both education and information technology became high-visibility national issues at the same time it was losing public revenue. Though the leaders decided to capitalize on the new opportunities, their decisions turned out to have serious unintended consequences. In a flurry of activity, new K-12 outreach programs were established as was the school's first revenue-generating doctoral program. Next was the merger of the former Graduate School of Library and Information Science, and Graduate School of Education into a new, two-department graduate school that promised even more new opportunities. At the same time, the school launched an aggressive development program, producing a substantial increase in private gifts. And as new funding opportunities for research on education and information technology became available, faculty members wrote a large number of proposals for support that produced a record number of grants and contracts.

No one foresaw that all this new activity would lead to hiring a large number of new adjunct faculty members (so called because they are nontenure-track or core faculty members). But while these new faculty members took on much responsibility for teaching and student mentoring, they were marginalized within the faculty community with none of the rights and privileges of the regular faculty. And they and the programs they belong to were not well integrated with the core faculty.

Faculty members in the Department of Physics and Astronomy struggled with huge reductions in federal grants, and with the increasing difficulty in recruiting good students. When we began the study in 1996, we were struck by many professors' gloomy assessment that the important problems of physics had already been solved and that the Cold War's end signaled the close of a golden era of science. But despite their colleagues' pessimistic outlook, department leaders recognized that there was no choice but to make changes and they rallied the faculty into an eleventh-hour turnaround.

An alliance with astronomy established in 1994 had already laid the groundwork for the new department to later expand into the growing fields of astrophysics and cosmology. With the expansion came a substantial increase in grant revenue, especially from astronomy. To attract more undergraduates, the department modernized the physics major. When UCLA's medical school threatened to teach its own physics courses the department feared losing the revenue and developed customized courses for students who must take physics courses for majors in chemistry, engineering, and life sciences.

While these findings reveal that universities do indeed change, the process is hard to manage and it is extraordinarily slow. It is slow because of the way universities were designed to stand apart from society as intellectual sanctuaries where ideas could be freely explored. But many of the very strategies designed to protect the university from interference insulate it from feedback that it needs to adapt.

Let us examine these old strategies and why they are flawed in today's environment. At the end of the chapter we will consider some new strategies to take their place and explore their implications for administrators and academic leaders.

Old Strategies

Buffer the Faculty from External Forces and Use the Practice of Shared Governance to Help Strengthen Faculty Autonomy.

Buffering is a time-tested strategy that is used successfully to protect universities' faculty from external intrusion. It works by vesting power in boundary agencies that manage exchanges with the larger environment. Buffering also allows boundary agencies to deflect incoming demands from an organization's technical core (Thompson, 1967; Scott, 1998). For instance, the University of California president's office uses functions like governmental relations, development, and public information to control exchanges across the university's boundaries. Because external demands must pass through these agencies, they serve to protect the faculty from political intrusion. Buffering extends to the campus level as well where the

University of California system-wide buffers are replicated. At UCLA, offices of governmental relations, public information, research administration, and development help manage demands from the larger environment.

A second strategy to strengthen faculty autonomy has been the use of shared governance, developed by the University of California in 1920 to balance academic and fiscal responsibility between the faculty and administration. Under shared governance, the faculty (represented by the academic senate) has final authority over curricular decisions, while the administration holds ultimate budget authority. While the academic and executive functions are divided, each side is obliged to consult with the other before making final decisions (Harrison, 1991).

Limits to buffering and shared governance. While buffering continues to protect the faculty, it also incurs serious costs by insulating the faculty from external realities. The practice of shared governance keeps responsibilities between the administration and faculty neatly drawn, but it also adds to the faculty's isolation. Added to the effects of buffering and shared governance is a lingering sense of mistrust between the faculty and administration. Some of the mistrust stems from differences in administrators' and faculty members' values. Administrators often joke about lazy professors who don't come to work until noon as faculty members disparage administrators as suits who are interested mainly in money. But mistrust is also an unintended outgrowth of shared governance, the spirit of which is to settle conflicts through consultation. But in the past, power has often been used to resolve conflict. An example was the 1993 "Professional Schools' Restructuring Initiative" that split the UCLA faculty over the administration's decision to close and reorganize a group of professional schools. While the senate ultimately voted for the restructuring, its leaders were branded as sellouts to the administration. Coupled with the shock of the decision itself, longstanding tensions between the faculty and the administration (that dated back to the loyalty oath controversy that had rocked the University of California in the early 1950s) became strained. The decision deepened suspicions that, as was the case in the 1950s, the administration had abandoned fundamental academic values for the sake of political or economic expediency.

The real limitation in buffering and shared governance is that together they tend to remove the faculty from feedback from the environment that carries important information about changing conditions. For instance, annual budget negotiations between the university and the governor, legislators' impressions of the university, and private philanthropy each have a serious impact on how the university operates. But, to most faculty members, the annual budget negotiation is a distant affair that has little to do with campus life. Recall how just a year after UCLA encountered its largest deficit in history ($110 million) a faculty member in a focus group convened to explore faculty attitudes replied, "What crisis? There's no crisis here." Recall the case of UCLA's attempt to implement Responsibility Center Management (RCM) that foundered in the face of faculty resistance. Many faculty leaders distrusted the administration and felt that it had overstated the economic crisis and had used RCM as an excuse to intrude into academic affairs. The accumulated years of distrust made it impossible for accommodations to be made, and the initiative died.

Insulating the faculty so effectively also constrains the university's ability to manage the inexorable trend toward privatization. Consider the fact that the mid 1960s, about 44% of UCLA's total budget came from state funds, but today only about 20% comes from the public purse. During the same period, the UCLA budget has increased nearly 20 times, from $116 million in 1965-1966 to more than $2 billion in 1997-1998, producing even more demands for private sources of support. As a result, UCLA has been required to develop new strategies to protect state funding and build the needed infrastructure to generate new private funds. It has been anything but easy.

UCLA, especially as part of a multi-campus public university, finds itself at a disadvantage compared to its faster moving private counterparts. Faculty members at private institutions like the University of Southern California (USC) or the

California Institute of Technology (CalTech) are more keenly aware of their institutions' financial outlook. As a result, they are more able to consider solutions to the thorny problems that accompany private gifts. The recent case of the Swiss pharmaceutical company Novartis and the University of California, Berkeley provides a useful glimpse of just how vexing these financial transactions can be (Press &Washburn, 2000). Novartis offered to pay UC Berkeley $25 million for basic research in its College of Natural Resources. In return, UC Berkeley agreed to give Novartis licensing rights and seats on its research committee. The proposal produced an outcry among the faculty, more than half of whom believed that the university was compromising its academic reputation.

Or recall the case of multimillionaire inventor, Alfred Mann, who in 1990 decided to give his alma mater, UCLA, $100 million to establish a biomedical institute to turn scientific discoveries into useful products. Mann said, "I want to create a bridge between academia and the industry (Dickerson & Weiss, 1998). But creating such a bridge presented an insurmountable obstacle to the UCLA administration and faculty. They argued over the influence Mann's gift would have on the direction of research, how royalties would be divided, and whether the institute would be housed in the medical school or the school of engineering. By 1998, Mann had become frustrated by the inaction and decided instead to give the money to UCLA's crosstown rival, the private University of Southern California. Though Mann says he still hopes to make a gift to UCLA, he added, "I didn't know it would be so much work giving money away."

To be fair, establishing partnerships between private companies and public universities is complex. Most university faculty members regard their research as a public good that must remain free of vested interests. And partnerships like those proposed by Novartis and Alfred Mann invariably encroach on this honored ground. But the reality is that private sector resources will continue to be sought and adjustments will have to be found to meet the needs of both donors and universities. But sheltering the faculty and removing them from fiscal responsibility will surely prolong the search for solutions.

Treat Academic Units as Uniform and Assume They Respond to External Demands in a Similar Fashion.

Historically, administrators have assumed that academic units were more similar than not and have treated them accordingly. Especially at large multi-campus universities like the University of California, policy issues that govern issues as diverse as faculty salaries and promotions, new academic programs, and student fees are developed through an unwieldy committee process. UCLA, like its sister campuses, is burdened with bureaucratic rules that have accreted over the years. Many regulations that treat academic programs alike not only slow decision-making to a glacial pace, but they also dampen innovative impulses. While exceptions have been made to accommodate self-supporting programs like Anderson's and the Graduate School of Education's, regulations still place heavy indirect costs on these programs and dictate campus services that must be used and paid for even though they may be inappropriate or inefficient.

Weakness in a "one-size-fits-all" strategy. Even this examination of three academic units reveals just how varied the university really is. In the same institution, academic units can be as different from each other as day is from night. And, as we saw in these cases, differences in units' cultures and organizational structures, and their relationship to markets, make profound differences in how they respond to external changes. It is anything but a homogeneous organization.

On one extreme is the Anderson School, mirroring corporate values—it is a well-run school that has an orderly and businesslike feel. Professors observe regular working hours. The floors in the impressive new building are polished, the windows are clean, and classrooms are neat. Financial incentives are important motivators to many Anderson faculty members. The Anderson School faculty unabashedly defines students as customers because student payments (tuition and fees) finance much of the school's operations.

The Graduate School of Education and Information Studies serves the educational and informational needs of public education, higher education, libraries, and governmental agencies. In contrast to the Anderson faculty, the GSE&IS faculty resist the idea of students as customers because the concept conflicts with their altruistic values that define students as co-producers of learning. Most of the school's financial support comes from third parties—foundations and government agencies—that the faculty does not consider customers.

On the other extreme is the Department of Physics and Astronomy, located in the College of Letters and Sciences, well within the traditional core of the university. Its culture and work processes would be strangers to the Anderson School, though less so to the Graduate School of Education and Information Studies. Faculty members are dedicated to the pursuit of fundamental questions about matter and the universe and are largely indifferent to external economic and political events that affect the university except when the survival of the unit is threatened. As in the Graduate School of Education and Information Studies, financial support comes from third parties—mostly from the federal government.

The implication is that profound differences in academic units' cultures, incentives, opportunities and constraints make it difficult to change the university with any one-size-fits-all policy. For instance, while RCM worked in the Anderson School, it was met with great resistance in others. This is not to say that uniform policies are unimportant. It is a public university, and each of its academic units operates in environments that are constrained to one degree or another. University rules and procedures buffer the academic core from external forces, and they provide checks and balances to mitigate misguided action. But they also have the negative effect of stifling the creation of new organizational forms, programs, and services. Results from this study make clear that to maximize the potential of academic units that are so distinct from one another, campus policies need to be tailored to the local variations in units' cultures and the environments in which they operate.

Protect the Core Academic Disciplines by Positioning Professional Schools on the Margins of the University.

This time-tested strategy grows out of the very design of the university in which the traditional disciplines—the physical and life sciences, social sciences, and humanities—comprise the academic core. This organizational form was taken from the German university that placed inquiry at its center (Clark, 1995; Rudolph, 1962). UCLA education professor Burton Clark describes the German university as the only institution in the world "in which a student could obtain training in how to do scientific or scholarly research" (Clark, 1995). Protecting scientific inquiry from interference was important. Radical economist Thorstein Veblen believed that scholars and scientists had to be actually isolated from society's influences (Veblen, 1957).

But the 19th century American university found it impossible to stand apart from society's demands as the country expanded. But how to protect the academic core from external influences? In a textbook case of organizational adaptation, professional schools were positioned outside of the traditional disciplinary core of the university. Historian Frederick Rudolph observed how the American university spawned "appropriate schools at appropriate times whether they were schools of business administration, forestry, journalism, veterinary medicine…" (Rudolph, 1962). From this position they could help the university achieve its ever-broadening educational mission and protect the traditional disciplines as centers of inquiry by bridging the distance between the university and the professions. Today, the strategy can be seen in the development of partnerships, joint ventures, and other cooperative ventures between the professional schools and external agencies.

Limits to the strategy of bridging. While bridging society's demands with universities' professional schools still makes sense, it ignores the needs of core academic units that have been well protected and lack the capacity for balancing external demands with internal requirements. The high-profile case of Novartis and UC Berkeley, and UCLA's loss of a $100 million gift from inventor Alfred Mann, illustrate the complexity of these new requirements. In today's resource-hungry environment, the importance of the market-model university is sure to grow. But its resource driven impulses will need to be tempered by new internal arrangements that better balance the needs for resources and traditional academic protections.

Administrators cannot forge and implement these new relationships alone because faculty members must ultimately approve them. The sooner that faculty members assume responsibility for and develop experience in attracting private resources, the easier changes that lie ahead will be.

But using the old strategy of bridging that looks to professional schools where these transactions occur more naturally, misses an opportunity to familiarize a larger number of faculty members to external reality. There is little doubt that faculty members in the traditional disciplines will, like their colleagues at UC Berkeley when the Novartis issue sufaced, find themselves increasingly drawn into decisions about accepting private gifts. And, in some cases they will find it in their own self-interest to generate funds from external sources. In both cases, universities and their core faculty members have much to learn from a close examination of how successful professional schools manage these exchanges.

Disregard Feedback from the Environment.

In a steady state environment, disregarding feedback about changing conditions, and how end users evaluate the university's products may have made more sense than it does today. Teaching and research existed in relatively stable environments in which resources were usually dependable, and labor markets for graduates were established and predictable. But in the last decade, as environments have become more turbulent and less predictable, feedback about changing conditions, and what they indicate about modifications in universities outputs and work processes, have now become of paramount importance.

Importance of feedback. Lacking feedback from output markets deprives universities of important signals that can help adjust research and teaching to changing external conditions.

We have discussed how organizations that function as open systems use feedback from their environments to help them adapt. One use of feedback, called single-loop learning, uses feedback to self-correct like a sailor who uses navigational data to keep a boat on course. Another use of feedback, called double-loop learning, uses the data to question existing goals (Argyris & Schon, 1978). Using data in this way may lead to entirely new goals, and when necessary, a fundamentally different direction.

Without feedback, organizations have trouble navigating through rapid changes because they lack information to gauge progress toward their goals or to question whether existing goals are still appropriate. In the ideal world, organizations develop the capability to scan and anticipate changes in their environments, question and change existing goals and assumptions, and encourage new patterns of organizational behavior. They learn how to internalize double-loop learning and avoid getting trapped in single-loop processes (Senge, 1990).

But the processes of buffering the faculty, bridging exchanges with professional schools, separating finance and academics through shared governance, and traditions of tenure, tend to minimize the importance of feedback to the faculty. For instance, the process of teaching (except in the Anderson School) is insensitive to feedback from output markets. Lacking this feedback makes it difficult for faculty members to adjust programs to consider end-users' (students and employers) demands. And there is little feedback from users of research that is conducted in the professional schools because much of it never reaches the field. The dominance of the traditional scientific model in the university's promotional system encourages professional school faculty members to conform to a narrow concept of research. Consequently, much of the professional school research is written for academic journals rather than for practitioners. But with a few exceptions, like the *Harvard Business Review*, few practitioners read these academic journals.

At the campus level, UCLA is rich in information, most of which is collected by the central administration (information on student enrollments, time-to-degree and graduation rates, faculty hiring and retention, costs and revenues, and student satisfaction). But, most of it (like the unused exit surveys of UCLA doctoral graduates) is not shared with academic units that could use it to make improvements in their programs.

At the unit level, we discovered a wide array of feedback loops. Some carried important information to decision-makers, while others were broken. In some places where feedback loops might be expected, they were nonexistent. For instance, Anderson School academic leaders have up-to-date feedback on costs and revenues and on student performance as well as their evaluations of the teaching program. One faculty member exclaimed, "Feedback loops are all over the place. They hit us in the face every time we turn around!" In GSE&IS's revenue-driven Educational Leadership Program, feedback on revenues and costs, student performance, and teaching quality is used regularly. But with that exception, feedback loops are hard to find in either GSE&IS or the Department of Physics and Astronomy. Student evaluations of instructors are usually not used for the purposes of improvement. Surveys of student perceptions are conducted sporadically within the two units but results are rarely shared with individual faculty members.

Feedback, or the lack of it, are significant clues to the many different ways that academic units think about their environments, their customers, and their internal operations. What is most obvious is that feedback occurs, but only when it is needed. During this study, both the Anderson School and the Department of Physics and Astronomy faced serious threats to their survival. We found plenty of evidence that both units actually used feedback effectively to engage in double-loop learning.

Use Top-down Strategic Planning to Align Campus Interests.

In theory, strategic planning can help a campus make effective choices among missions and align the faculty and administration in a common purpose. As we discussed in Chapter One, strategic planning is a concept borrowed from private industry, but it usually fails when applied in a university environment. Thousands of colleges and universities have undertaken strategic planning in the last decade. But, according to one authority, only a few institutions have "transformed themselves dramatically... many institutions have stumbled, dissolved into controversy, or lost their nerve" (Keller, 1997).

Shortcomings of top-down planning. Results from our study bear out these observations. We saw how strategic planning usually fails to penetrate the ranks of the faculty where the changes must occur. For instance, UCLA administrators realized that Responsibility Center Management (RCM) was failing and turned to strategic planning. Deans were required to develop plans and submit them to higher-level administrators for consideration and approval. However, we found little evidence that this top-down process had much impact below the dean level. For instance, in the Graduate School of Education and Information Studies, where the faculty was unaware of an external threat, the interim dean and the chairs of both departments talked with the faculty about the chancellor's vision and the need for strategic planning. Yet the faculty remained largely unconcerned and disinterested and no substantive changes resulted from the exercise.

Since then, this kind of planning has expanded to the entire campus. As might be expected, it has become a process that is important to the deans and the academic units, because resources are allocated partly on the basis of their plans. But, more often than not, strategic plans have little bearing on desires of individual faculty members, most of whom remain detached from the process. Most take comfort in the fact that their autonomy will allow them, within reason, to do whatever they want. One dean described the strategic planning process as pure fiction. He added, "My staff and I make up these wonderful plans, but they don't have much to do with what's going on. But they keep the funds flowing."

Our findings suggest an alternative to the traditional top-down strategic planning. We saw ample evidence of how the faculty can respond vigorously when it senses a serious threat or new opportunity. Recall when the Anderson School was facing a serious threat to its survival; the faculty invented a voluntary form of strategic planning. Under great pressure from declining national rankings, senior members of the faculty began meeting to identify the scope of the problem and to analyze alternative future directions for the school. Another voluntary version of strategic planning also occurred in the Department of Physics and Astronomy when the faculty realized its future was in jeopardy. Professors voluntarily scanned the environment for new and promising scientific opportunities, such as biophysics, astrophysics, and cosmology, while creating new curricular offerings for the medical school and the undergraduate physics major. In both cases, faculty members were able to implement significant changes that the administration could not have done alone. But because academic units operate in relative isolation with little communication between one another, this voluntary planning goes on unnoticed and it is not institutionalized.

New Strategies

Let us now turn to a discussion of how lessons from this study can help administrators and academic leaders make the process of change more conscious and deliberate. These new strategies are intended to help administrators and academic leaders more fully realize the educational power found in their institutions' human resources. The following strategies are not simplistic prescriptions about what leaders should or should not do. Rather, they strive to unite the collective interests of faculty and administration while striking a balance with valuing and protecting individual academic freedom. We take confidence in their usefulness because we witnessed them actually in use. Though they existed as fragmented and voluntary efforts, these strategies represented successful adaptations made by administrators and faculty members.

Let us discuss each of them and then turn to a broader discussion of their implications for managing change.

Expose the Faculty to Changing Economic and Political Forces that Affect the University.

There is growing evidence that too much buffering can be a bad thing. While buffering the traditional academic core may temporarily protect the faculty from interference, it also ensures that it will be out of touch with the environment. No organization can succeed in today's fast changing and competitive world if its products or services do not satisfy its customers' needs and expectations. Nor can it succeed if it has no way of modifying its products or services on the basis of user feedback. As this study demonstrates, the faculty must be exposed to regular feedback from students and others who use the results of their work, as well as to economic and political trends that affect their institutions. The challenge is finding the right balance between maintaining faculty autonomy and engagement in activities that have formerly been reserved for administrators.

One part of the strategy is to reduce the buffers that exist between university stakeholders and the faculty. Sometimes buffers are reduced by the emergence of powerful new opportunities. For instance, California universities have witnessed a growing demand for faculty members' knowledge to help educate the waves of new legislators produced by a voter initiative that limited legislators' terms. The same initiative cut deeply into the legislature's consultant staff, making legislators more dependent than ever on knowledgeable faculty members for expert advice from their research.

Another part of the strategy is to reinterpret divisions in responsibilities between the faculty and administration. The University of California's practice of shared governance is a formalized version of the division of fiscal and academic matters that many campuses face. It is the responsibility of the faculty leadership to ensure that faculty members begin to grasp their units' fiscal reality if they are to influence it. The idea expressed by one faculty member, who said about the budget, "That's not my business; I'm not paid to be an accountant," needs a close reexamination.

Observe How Professional Schools Manage the Bridging Function and Diffuse the Learnings to More Protected Academic Units.

Because professional schools encounter environmental changes sooner than do the traditional disciplines at the university's academic core, they can alert university leaders to changes and help them buy time to consider their implications. For instance, the Anderson School's declining national rankings set off a chain of rapid activity that ultimately required correction. It also required a reexamination of the school's mission and how its work processes supported its mission. In another example, the GSE&IS's Educational Leadership Program had to provide education of sufficiently high quality that students would pay substantially higher tuition than regular graduate students. Because self-supporting programs like these must be sensitive to their customers, they can help university faculties consider how to be responsive to students' changing needs while nurturing independent critical thought.

Professional schools are well designed and positioned to be scouts for new ideas because of exchanges their faculty members make with external agencies—business and labor organizations, government agencies, school districts, hospitals, and libraries. The university as a whole can benefit and derive enhanced economic and political support from these schools' innovations. Individual academic units, particularly those that have been sheltered from market forces, and have less experience responding to demands from the external environment, can learn from successful professional schools.

Build on the Diversity of Academic Units and Allow for Variation in Policies and the Emergence of Innovative Organizational Forms and Strategies.

The university is anything but homogeneous. Former University of California president Clark Kerr described it as a multiversity with multiple units, each with its own set of constraints, opportunities, incentives, and constituencies. Each unit responds differently to external threats and opportunities through a cultural lens that supports and directs its activity. The academic units' cultures also reflect their environments and how they define their customers. Except for universal beliefs in academic freedom, faculty autonomy, and rational thought, the cultures and work processes of these three units are extraordinarily different from one another.

While overall policies are needed to ensure the university serves a common vision and mission, university strategy should encourage diverse academic units to capitalize on their strengths and unique qualities. For example, academic leaders should examine the wisdom of evaluating research produced by professional schools using criteria derived from the traditional sciences. New policies that redefined research outcomes as impact on professional practice could connect professional schools and their professions more productively. New policies that encouraged the development of self-supporting programs by creating incentives for faculty members could also forge new and productive relationships between the university and external agencies.

In any case, decisions like these must be made by faculty members who are closest to the research, teaching, and public service, and who best know their units' strengths and weaknesses. This study revealed how quickly the faculty can become engaged if they are convinced that their investment of time and effort will be valued. Further, by encouraging new ideas to emanate from the faculty, the rate of innovation and adaptation will increase, as will the faculty commitment to new programmatic directions.

Build Faculty-Designed Feedback Loops into Academic Units that Indicate Modifications in Core Processes.

Engaging the faculty to develop feedback loops that carry reliable and useful information to their academic units is a starting point. The study showed that once feedback was required, as it was in the Anderson School, it became commonplace. And once faculty members recognized the impact of their actions, they were likely to modify their behavior when changes were indicated.

An analogy may help make the point. In the 1970s, houses in a New Jersey development were equipped with measuring devices at each point where energy was used. Hot and cold water, furnaces, lights, and appliances like refrigerators and televisions, were each outfitted with simple gauges that told users how much energy they were using. Energy use plummeted (Harrigan, Kempton, & Ramakrishna, 1995). That experiment has been repeated many times over, showing that as residents discovered negative consequences of their actions, they quickly modified their behavior.

New policies could make the faculty in academic units responsible for identifying key indicators of progress toward their goals. Measures might include student performance and completion rates, the quality of faculty teaching, the volume of proposals for contracts and grants and the financial yield, the impact of faculty research, and so forth. Data could be generated annually and shared with other units. To ensure accountability and to aid in planning for the university as a whole, it would also be shared with top administrators and academic leaders. Producing information to reveal academic units' strengths and weaknesses—that could also be shared with the larger university community—would in all likelihood produce voluntary faculty participation. We take confidence in this suggestion from the widespread altruism and rationality found among the faculty. This information would also reveal disparities between academic units' goals and their progress, and it would indicate corrective to be taken.

Having information of this kind would also help academic units exert more control over their own destinies. Too often, academic leaders say that information produced by the central administration on their units is often either incorrect or outdated. Deciding for themselves on important descriptors and performance measures would enable leaders to portray their units accurately. It would also save time they now spend defending themselves against misperceptions caused by incorrect data.

Lead Strategic Planning Simultaneously from the Top of the Organization and the Bottom.

There is little doubt that changes in the environment will only intensify. This is not the first time that the university has been pressed to change. Rudolph writes how late 19th century universities were so pressured by society that "every institution knew that it had to do something, even if necessary, defend its right to stand still" (Rudolph, 1962). But this is the first time that changes have come so quickly. The impact of an international economy and the use of new technologies will most certainly continue to reshape the country's labor market and its economy. At the same time, population demographics are predicted to continue to shift and under-represented groups will keep up pressure for inclusion in the university. Increasing demands for revenue will most likely be met in large part by the private sector; that will intensify pressures to create the market-model university.

Most observers agree that planning has become an essential tool to help universities adapt to the changes and continue to meet society's needs but admit that it rarely succeeds. Top-down planning that fails to fully engage employees does not work. This is especially true of universities, where professionals manage the technical core. Yet this problem is a difficult one to solve. There is little question that the process has to be led by top administrative and academic leaders. But it must be embraced and energized by rank-and-file faculty members with their own ideas and insights because in the end they must legitimate the process. Without their full participation, faculty members will remain uncommitted to any new direction, and their lack of commitment will undermine even the best efforts. Planning and implementing changes that enable institutions of higher education to adapt must become integral and indispensable or they will continue to be dismissed by faculty members as marginal exercises.

Managing Change

These findings make it abundantly clear how the university's organizational structure and its underlying culture make it difficult to respond to changes in the environment. Being organized as a loosely-coupled bureaucracy, in which power is widely dispersed, makes it difficult enough. And while decision making is not as nonrational as Lindblom's conception of "muddling through" suggests, it is nonlinear and slow (Lindblom, 1959). When one takes into consideration the additional fact that university employees are professionals who are insulated from external pressures by traditions of tenure and shared governance, it is little wonder that change occurs at all.

Many books and articles have been written on strategic planning in higher education (see Chaffee, 1989; Lawler, 1986; Mills & Pumo, 1999; Tierney, 1999 to name a few). They contain the usual litany of actions academic leaders must take—establishing a sense of urgency, forming coalitions, creating and communicating a vision, empowering others, and so on. But most of these prescriptions fail to consider why planning fails and what might be done to enlist the faculty and the administration in a common effort.

The reasons for its failure are obvious. Recall that new faculty members are already socialized to expect academic freedom and autonomous working conditions. As employed professionals, they are buffered from external realities by their own universities, they work in organizations where power is widely dispersed, and decisions take a nonlinear path. As faculty members are promoted, they become further insulated by traditions of tenure that translate into job protection. The effect is to isolate faculty members from the very pressures that are needed to help universities adapt to constantly changing conditions.

Some academics write about change in higher education by drawing overly simplified analogies from industry, suggesting that reengineering be used to create high performance colleges and universities (Tierney, 1999). But what this point of view fails to grasp is that change does not occur voluntarily even in private corporations. Many of them have to be driven beyond the brink of disaster before they can respond. And then, only some survive.

Companies that we have studied over many years taught a lesson of signal importance. No strategic action is possible until employees at all levels of an organization recognize external threats (Wilms, 1996; Zell, 1997). Kurt Lewin and Edgar Schein understood the truth in this statement years ago when each wrote about the difficulty of shaking organizations out of their fearful paralysis (Lewin, 1951; Schein, 1985).

Despite the proliferation of books that promise to create adaptive organizational cultures, they are never created voluntarily. Nor is this kind of change painless. From his observation of indigenous people, anthropologist Bronislaw Malinowski reminds us that cultures always emerge as adaptations to changing environments (Malinowski, 1927). Later, industrial psychologist Kurt Lewin recognized the necessity of unfreezing organizations before meaningful change could occur (Lewin, 1951). What Lewin meant is that all members of an organization had to feel the need to change before change could take place because of the discomfort it produces. The accuracy of Lewin's observation has been validated repeatedly.

Even in the industrial world, a collective myopia has doomed more than one company. John McDonnell, chairman of McDonnell Douglas (that has since been absorbed by Boeing), acknowledged that he wished he had moved to reform its giant subsidiary, Douglas Aircraft, more quickly. But he and his executives failed to see the warning signs until it was too late. They also seriously misjudged the power of Douglas's underlying culture that prevented employees and managers from taking action. Even among companies that succeeded in responding in time, wrenching pain was needed to drive home the truth. General Motors had to close its Fremont plant, throwing nearly 6,000 men and women out of work before the cycle of destructiveness could be broken and NUMMI could be established. Hewlett-Packard's venerated Santa Clara division had to face imminent failure before it could respond by redesigning its core work processes from top to bottom.

Does It Take a Crisis to Change?

Let us now return to our original question. Do colleges and universities have to be in a crisis before they can respond and change? Before conducting this study we believed the answer was yes. We were convinced that only a huge shock could get the faculty's attention. We were reminded of President Harry Truman's quip that the best way to get a mule's attention was to hit it in the head with a two-by-four. But using coercive force is not a productive strategy in any institution, least of all in the university. As we have seen, university faculties have a remarkable capacity to rationalize and deflect even the most serious blows. Consider how faculty members have reacted in case after case to heavy-handed tactics by university executives bent on removing tenure or dismantling programs.

Even when pressure for change comes from the inside where the faculty can control its direction, resistance can be remarkable. A recent study of 26 colleges and universities that were attempting to transform themselves revealed that most faculty members and administrators were "...not convinced of the need for transformation and were leery of the risks involved." Campus leaders said they could not advocate changes, "...without creating deep anxiety and alienating people who were central to implementing the change" (Eckel, Hill, & Green, 1998). We observed this kind of resistance closely in 1993 when we began a discussion in UCLA's Graduate School of Education and Information Studies about redesigning the core processes to help the school better focus its resources on teaching and research in ways the faculty deemed important. UCLA had just been faced with a $110 million deficit—the largest in its history. The new dean quickly saw the implications of Hewlett-Packard's experience with organizational redesign for higher education. He invited the company's redesign expert to meet with the faculty executive committee. In the abstract. everyone agreed that embarking on a redesign was a good idea. But when a formal proposal was made to the faculty executive committee, its members balked. The members defended their position with comments like, "We're number one. There's nothing broken to fix." "We don't want any fads from industry. This is a priestly occupation, and these corporate ideas are offensive. Anyway, there's no crisis here." The idea died quickly, the economy rebounded, and resources again began to flow, obscuring any memory of a problem.

Much has already been written about the steps of strategic planning, and we have no wish to repeat them here (see Hax & Majluf, 1996; Hunger & Wheelen, 2001). What is abundantly clear is that without the commitment of the faculty, the process is meaningless. But gaining this commitment is another matter. We have reported on the persistent sense of mistrust that lies submerged between the faculty and administration. The roots of this antipathy lie buried in history and in the very design of the American university and the professoriate. While the creation of shared governance years earlier by the University of California seemed to have solved the problem by assigning responsibilities to the faculty and administration, mistrust has resurfaced. No doubt a renewed sensitivity stems from external pressures that threaten the existing order.

A typical reaction is for the faculty to become defensive. At a meeting of the Social Science Research Council discussed earlier where we previewed this study's conclusions and recommendations with scholars of higher education, we were surprised at the energetic attack. One concern was that by using data to plan and implement organizational changes, the university would be reduced to an economic institution to satisfy its customers. The case of the Anderson School truly worried scholars who fear such a market-driven model will come to represent all of higher education. Part of academics' worry in starting down the path of change is that the university's operations will become transparent. One respected scholar said candidly, "I'm not sold on transparency. I'm in favor of some useful mystification." He added, "Adopting a consumer model for higher education where transactions are transparent can break down faculty authority."

However appealing this position may be, it seems headed in the wrong direction because both faculties and their universities will be the losers. There is already a palpable concern among many academics that the business of the university has pushed too far into the academic core. Stanford education professor Patricia Gumport writes that professors are increasingly regarded by administrators as "employees, potential revenue sources, resources to be redeployed, and competitors rather than colleagues" (Gumport, 1997). Gumport concludes that faculty members must listen to "external pressures but be ardent in their advocacy of intangible but essential values."

UCLA higher education professors, Alexander Astin and Helen Astin, who studied the 26 colleges and universities that were attempting to transform themselves, are convinced that faculty members' very autonomy may be the key. They write, "While autonomy can be misused, it is also one of our greatest potential assets for initiating change" (Astin & Astin, 2000). Results of our investigation of UCLA have led us to a similarly upbeat viewpoint.

Our hope is that faculty leaders will be able to begin a conversation with colleagues about establishing a new and powerful voice in the affairs of the university. Rather than stepping back into the shadows of an opaque and mysterious university, they can lead a new effort to create a visible process of data-gathering, planning, implementation, evaluation, and adjustment for which they are accountable, but over which they retain substantial control.

Results of this research lead to a new and hopeful perspective. Colleges and universities already have within them the needed ingredients to become greater contributors in a rapidly changing world. What is needed is a reexamination of some key assumptions and new strategies to help in this period of transition. In the course of this research, we have become convinced that faculty action is possible in the absence of a crisis.

But changes cannot be forced by administrators. As French philosopher Jean-Jacques Rousseau observed in 1762, and as we have seen in modern-day efforts to alter higher education, the unilateral use of force produces change that is far less durable than voluntarily action. Changes that are now required will have to be made in cooperation with the faculty if they are to endure.

References

Argyris, C., & Schon, D. A. (1978). *Organizational learning: A theory of action perspective.* Reading, MA: Addison-Wesley.

Astin, A., & Astin, H. (2000). *Leadership reconsidered: Engaging higher education in social change.* Battle Creek, MI: W. K. Kellogg Foundation.

Chaffee, E. E. (1989). Strategy and effectiveness in systems of higher education. In J. Smart (Ed.), *Higher education: Handbook of theory and research: Vol. 1.* New York, NY: Agathon.

Clark, B. R. (1995). Complexity and differentiation: The deepening problem of integration. In D. D. Dill and B. Sporn (Eds.), *Emerging patterns of social demand and university reform: Through a glass darkly.* Oxford, England: Pergamon.

Clark, B. (1993). *The higher education system: Academic organization in cross-national perspective.* Berkeley, CA: University of California Press.

Dickerson, M., & Weiss, K. R. (1998, February 5). Entrepreneur to donate $100 Million to USC. *Los Angeles Times,* p. A1.

Eckel, P., Hill, B., & Green, M. (1998). *On change: En route to transformation.* Washington, DC: American Council on Education.

Gumport, P. (1997). Public universities as academic workplaces. *Daedalus, 126* (4), 113-136.

Harrigan, M., Kempton, W., & Ramakrishna, V. (1995). *Empowering customer energy choices: A review of personal interaction and feedback in energy efficient programs.* Washington, DC: The Alliance to Save Energy.

Harrison, B. (1991). *Shared governance.* Unpublished paper. Santa Barbara, CA: University of California.

Hax, A., & Majluf, N. (1996). *The strategy concept and process.* Upper Saddle River, NJ: Prentice Hall.

Hunger, J. D., & Wheelen T. (2001). *Essentials of strategic management*. Upper Saddle River, NJ: Prentice Hall.

Keller, G. (1997). Foreword. In D. Rowley, H. Lujan, & M. Dolence (Eds.), *Strategic change in colleges and universities* (pp. *ix-xi*). San Francisco, CA: Jossey-Bass.

Lawler, E. (1986). *High involvement management*. San Francisco, CA: Jossey-Bass.

Lewin, K. (1951). *Field theory in social science: Selected theoretical papers*. New York, NY: Harper and Row.

Lindblom, E. (1959, Spring). The science of muddling through. *Public Administration Review*, pp. 79-88.

Malinowki, B. (1927). The life of culture. In G. E. Smith, B. Malinowski, H. Spinden, & A. Goldenweiser (Eds.), *Culture: The diffusion controversy*. New York, NY: Norton.

Mills, D. Q., & Pumo, J. M. (1999). Managing change in higher education: A leader's guide. In D. Oblinger & R. Katz (Eds.), *Renewing administration*. Bolton, MA: Anker.

Press, E., & Washburn, J. (2000, March). The kept university. *The Atlantic Monthly, 285* (3).

Rudolph, F. (1962). *The American college and university*. New York, NY: Vintage.

Schein, E. (1985). *Organizational culture and leadership*. San Francisco, CA: Jossey-Bass.

Scott, W. R. (1998). *Organizations: Rational, natural, and open systems*. Upper Saddle River, NJ: Prentice Hall.

Senge, P. (1990). *The fifth discipline*. New York, NY: Doubleday.

Thompson, J. D. (1967). *Organizations in action*. New York, NY: McGraw Hill.

Tierney, W. G. (1999). *Building the responsive campus: Creating high performance colleges and universities*. Thousand Oaks, CA: SAGE Publications.

Veblen, T. (1957). *Higher learning in America*. New York, NY: Hill and Wang.

Wilms, W. W. (1996). *Restoring prosperity: How workers and managers are forging a new culture of cooperation*. New York, NY: Random House.

Zell, D. M. (1997). *Changing by design: Work innovation at Hewlett-Packard*. Ithaca, NY: Cornell University Press.

Bibliography

Abel, D. (2000, December 28). Measuring what college students learn proves elusive. *The Boston Globe,* p. 1.

Astin, A., & Astin, H. (2000). *Leadership reconsidered: Engaging higher education in social change.* Battle Creek, MI: W.K. Kellogg Foundation.

Argyris, C., & Schon, D. A. (1978). *Organizational learning: A theory of action perspective.* Reading, MA: Addison-Wesley.

Birnbaum, R. (1991). The latent organization functions of the academic senate: Why senates do not work but will not go away. In R. Birnbaum (Ed.), *Faculty in governance: The role of senates and joint committees in academic decision making.* New Directions for Higher Education, No. 75. San Francisco, CA: Jossey-Bass.

Bronner, E. (1999, June 5). U of Chicago president to return to teaching. *New York Times,* p. A10.

Brownstein, A. (2000, October 27). Tuition rises faster than inflation, and faster than in previous year. *The Chronicle of Higher Education,* p. A50.

Callis, D. (2001). *Storming the ivory tower.* Unpublished paper, Harvard Business School, Cambridge, MA.

Cameron, K. (1984). Organizational adaptation and higher education. *Journal of Higher Education,* 55 (2), 122-144.

Chaffee, E. E. (1989). Strategy and effectiveness in systems of higher education. In J. Smart (Ed.), *Higher education: Handbook of theory and research: Vol. 1.* New York, NY: Agathon.

Clark, B. R. (1995). Complexity and differentiation: The deepening problem of integration. In D. D. Dill and B. Sporn (Eds.), *Emerging patterns of social demand and university reform: Through a glass darkly.* Oxford, England: Pergamon.

Clark, B. (1993). *The higher education system: Academic organization in cross-national perspective.* Berkeley, CA: University of California Press.

Clayton, M. (2001, January 2). Higher education's undercurrents. *The Christian Science Monitor,* p. 10.

Clayton, M. (1999, June 29). Taking on 'sacred cows' in higher education. *The Christian Science Monitor,* p. 18.

Cohen, M. D., & March, J. G. (1976). Decisions, presidents, and status. In J. G. March & J. P. Olsen (Eds.), *Ambiguity and choice in organizations.* Bergen, Norway: Universitetsforlaget.

Cohen, M. D., March, J. G., & Olsten, J. P. (1972). A garbage can model of organizational choice. *Administrative Science Quarterly, 17,* 1-25.

College campuses will grow more diverse, report says. (2000, June 2). *The Chronicle of Higher Education*, p. A51.

Cyert, R., & March, J. G. (1992). *A behavioral theory of the firm* (2nd ed.). Englewood Cliffs, NJ: Prentice Hall.

Dickerson, M., & Weiss, K. R. (1998, February 5). Entrepreneur to donate $100 Million to USC. *Los Angeles Times*, p. A1.

Dill, D. D., & Sporn, B. (1995). University 2001: What will the university of the twenty-first century look like? In D. D. Dill & B. Sporn (Eds.), *Emerging patterns of social demand and university reform: Through a glass darkly.* Oxford: Pergamon.

DiMaggio, P. J., & Powell, W. W. (1983). The iron cage revisited: Institutional isomorphism and collective rationality in organizational fields. *American Sociological Review, 48,* 147-160.

Eckel, P., Hill, B., & Green, M. (1998). *On change: En route to transformation.* Washington, DC: American Council on Education.

Ehrenberg, R. (2000). *Why college costs so much.* Boston, MA: Harvard University Press.

Francis, D. (2000, January 18). Step right up for some higher education about the real costs of college. *The Christian Science Monitior*, p. 17.

Friedman, T. (1999, November 17). Foreign affairs: Next it's e-ducation. *The New York Times*, p. A25.

Gose, B. (1999, June 18). A president's controversial legacy. *The Chronicle of Higher Education*, p. A43.

Gumport, P. (1997). Public universities as academic workplaces. *Daedalus, 126* (4), 113-136.

Gumport, P., & Pusser, B. (1999). University restructuring: The role of economic and political contexts. In J. Smart & W. Tierney (Eds.), *Higher education: Handbook of theory and research, XIV.* New York, NY: Agathon.

Gumport, P. J., & Sporn, B. (1999). Institutional adaptation: Demands for management reform and university administration. In J. Smart & W. Tierney (Eds.), *Higher education: Handbook of theory and research, XIV.* New York, NY: Agathon.

Hannan, M., & Freeman, J. (1997). The population ecology of organization. *American Journal of Sociology, 82* (5), 929-964.

Hardy, C., Langley, A., Mintzberg, H., & Rose, J. (1984). Strategy formation in the university setting. In J. Bess (Ed.), *College and university organization: Insights for the behavioral sciences.* New York, NY: New York University Press.

Harrigan, M., Kempton, W., & Ramakrishna, V. (1995). *Empowering customer energy choices: A review of personal interaction and feedback in energy efficient programs.* Washington, DC: The Alliance to Save Energy.

Harrison, B. (1991). *Shared governance*. Unpublished paper. Santa Barbara, CA: University of California.

Hax, A., & Majluf, N. (1996). *The strategy concept and process*. Upper Saddle River, NJ: Prentice Hall.

Hunger, J. D., & Wheelen T. (2001). *Essentials of strategic management*. Upper Saddle River, NJ: Prentice Hall.

Keller, G. (1997). Foreword. In D. Rowley, H. Lujan, & M. Dolence (Eds.), *Strategic change in colleges and universities* (pp. *ix-xi*). San Francisco, CA: Jossey-Bass.

Lawler, E. (1986). *High involvement management*. San Francisco, CA: Jossey-Bass.

Lawrence, P., & Lorsch, J. (1967). Differentiation and integration in complex organizations. *Administrative Science Quarterly. 12*:1-47.

Lewin, K. (1951). *Field theory in social science: Selected theoretical papers*. New York, NY: Harper and Row.

Lindblom, E. (1959, Spring). The science of muddling through. *Public Administration Review*, 79-88.

Lively, K. (1999, February 26). U. of Florida's 'bank' rewards colleges that meet key goals. *The Chronicle of Higher Education*, p. A35.

Malinowki, B. (1927). The life of culture. In G. E. Smith, B. Malinowski, H. Spinden, & A. Goldenweiser (Eds.), *Culture: The diffusion controversy*. New York, NY: Norton.

Measuring Up 2000 (2000, November 30). National Center for public policy and higher education. San Jose, CA.

Mills, D. Q., & Pumo, J. M. (1999). Managing change in higher education: A leader's guide. In D. Oblinger & R. Katz (Eds.), *Renewing administration*. Bolton, MA: Anker.

Mintzberg, H. (1994). *The rise and fall of strategic planning*. New York, NY: Free Press.

Mintzberg, H., & Quinn, J. (1998). *Readings in the strategy process* (3rd ed.). Englewood Cliffs, NJ: Prentice Hall.

Olson, F. (1999, August 6). Virtual institutions challenge accreditors to devise new ways of measuring quality. *The Chronicle of Higher Education*, p. A29.

Pfeffer, J., & Salancik, G. (1978). *The external control of organizations: A resource dependence perspective*. New York, NY: Harper & Row.

Press, E., & Washburn, J. (2000, March). The kept university. *The Atlantic Monthly, 285* (3).

Quinn, J. B. (1978). *Strategies for change: Logical incrementalism*. Homewood, IL: Richard D. Irwin, Inc.

Rowley, D., Lujan, H., & Dolence, M. (1997). *Strategic change in colleges and universities*. San Francisco, CA: Jossey-Bass.

Rudolph, F. (1962). *The American college and university*. New York, NY: Vintage.

Schein, E. (1985). *Organizational culture and leadership*. San Francisco, CA: Jossey-Bass.

Scott, W. R. (1998). *Organizations: Rational, natural, and open systems*. Upper Saddle River, NJ: Prentice Hall.

Senge, P. (1990). *The fifth discipline*. New York, NY: Doubleday.

Stewart, G. R. (1971). *The year of the oath*. New York, NY: Da Copa Press.

Thompson, J. D. (1967). *Organizations in action*. New York, NY: McGraw Hill.

Tierney, W. G. (1999). *Buiding the responsive campus: Creating higher performance colleges and universities*. Thousand Oaks, CA: Sage Publications.

Veblen, T. (1957). *Higher learning in America*. New York, NY: Hill and Wang.

Weick, K. (1976, March). Educational organizations as loosely coupled systems. *Administrative Science Quarterly*.

Whalen, E. (1991). *Responsibility center management*. Bloomington, IN: Indiana University Press.

Wilms, W. W. (1996). *Restoring prosperity: How workers and managers are forging a new culture of cooperation*. New York, NY: Random House.

Wilson, J. Q. (1989). *Bureaucracy*. New York, NY: Basic Books.

Woodward, C. (2000, May 5). Worldwide tuition increases send students into the streets. *The Chronicle of Higher Education*, p. A54.

Zell, D. M. (1997). *Changing by design: Work innovation at Hewlett-Packard*. Ithaca, NY: Cornell Press.

Index